"Jan shows you how to make your a_
sets—regardless of your past or pre

Founder and Chairman of New Life Ministries
Author of *Every Man's Battle* and *Reframe Your Life*

"Jan Coates exudes positivity."

—Mary DeMuth
Author of *Thin Places: A Memoir*

"The book that changes your life. You will discover wherever you are emotionally, this book will rock your world."

—Lisa Copen, author
Beyond Casseroles: 505 Ways to Encourage a Chronically Ill Friend
Founder of RestMinistries.com

"Be prepared to get real, get raw, and get logical with yourself. It's a secret worth passing on."

—Eva Marie Everson
Author of *This Fine Life*

"It's packed with wisdom that will not only brighten your day but also transform your life."

—Linda Evans Shepherd, Author
When You Don't Know What to Pray,
How to Talk to God About Anything

"Bravo, Jan Coates! . . . Prepare to propel from surviving to thriving."

—Kay DeKalb Smith
International Speaker, Singer, Humorist

"Don't miss it. In fact, buy one for yourself and one for a friend."

—Karen O'Connor, Speaker
Author of best-selling books *Gettin' Old Ain't for Wimps* and
Help, Lord! I'm Having a Senior Moment

"It pinpoints real-life issues and gives practical advice for lasting change.
. . . This book is a must-read for women desiring a new outlook on life."

—Grace Fox
National Co-director of International Messengers Canada
International Speaker
Author of *Moving from Fear to Freedom:*
A Woman's Guide to Peace in Every Situation

"Her stories will touch you, her challenges will inspire you, and her secrets will change you."

—Vonda Skelton
National Speaker
Author of *Seeing Through the Lies: Unmasking the Myths Women Believe* and
The Bitsy Burroughs Mysteries

"*Attitude-inize* is a revelation to any of us who are trying to find the love and acceptance that God offers. Jan Coates is a courageous overcomer. Her book resonates with her joyful, positive voice."

—Suzie Humphreys
Award-winning International Motivational and Inspirational Humorist
Author of *If All Else Fails Laugh!*

"*Attitude-inize* is a life-changer for women who are ready to let go of the past and pursue their joy-filled, God-given future."

—Captain Heather Odom, MSW
Divisional Social Service Director
The Salvation Army

"*Attitude-inize* is a no-fluff attitude book that will nudge you out of your negativity zone."

—Carole Lewis
First Place 4 Health National Director
Author of *Give God a Year*

"*Attitude-inize* will uplift you, inspire you, and give you practical insight to develop a positive perspective in life."

—Karol Ladd
Author of *The Power of a Positive Woman*

"Through real stories interwoven with scripture, Jan Coates gives you the secrets to living a godly, abundant life."

Lieutenant Monica Contreras
Corps Officer
The Salvation Army

Jan Coates' journey from abused child to faith-filled woman in full-time ministry will inspire you to pursue the same optimistic approach to life that has served her so well. *Attitude-inize* shows the way!"

—Donna Partow
Best-selling author of *Becoming a Vessel God Can Use* and
Becoming the Woman God Wants Me to Be

Attitude-inize
10
SECRETS
TO A POSITIVE YOU

JAN COATES

BEACON HILL PRESS
OF KANSAS CITY

Library of Congress Cataloging-in-Publication Data

Coates, Jan.
   Attitude-inize : 10 secrets to a positive you / Jan Coates.
     p. cm.
   Includes bibliographical references.
   ISBN 978-0-8341-2611-4 (pbk.)
    1. Christian women—Religious life. 2. Attitude (Psychology)—Religious aspects—Christianity. 3. Christian women—Conduct of life. I. Title. II. Title: 10 secrets to a positive you III. Title: Ten secrets to a positive you.
   BV4527.C59 2011
   248.8'43—dc22

2010051629

10 9 8 7 6 5 4 3 2 1

CONTENTS

FOREWORD

The queen of good attitudes has written the book we all need to read—and what an honor to be asked to write its foreword! Seriously. When I first met Jan Coates I thought, *How can anyone be so happy and positive all the time? She must really lead a blessed life!*

Now that I know Jan better, I realize she truly does lead a blessed life—by choice. And it is that daily and sometimes moment-by-moment—choice that produces her positive and happy glow.

Jan is a been-there-done-that kind of gal. If you've got a hurt, she's probably felt it. If you're facing a tough challenge, chances are she's faced it too. If you're in the bottom of a pit with no visible way out, she's well acquainted with pits. Find that hard to believe? Here are some of the not-so-positive-or-pleasant issues Jan has encountered in her lifetime:

- Raised by a mentally ill mom.
- Endured a childhood filled with unthinkable abuse.
- Married at age seventeen—a divorced mom at nineteen.
- Experienced the death of her only biological child to a drunk driver.
- Battled depression.
- Faced life-threatening cancer.

Believe me now? Jan Coates knows about pain and discouragement, frustration and loss, challenges and disappointments. But through it all she's learned the secrets to overcoming them—and now she has summarized them in ten power-packed chapters to share with us. She also includes a bonus "tool kit" chapter. How amazing is that?

If you're up against something right now and you think you'll never get past it, if you've experienced a loss that has ripped your heart out and convinced you you'll never know joy again, if you've failed so many times you think there's a big "loser" tattoo on your forehead—you need to read this book. If you're a young married mom with never enough time or money or energy to get through the day/week/month, if you're a middle-aged woman whose dreams have seemingly evaporated into thin air, if you're a senior citizen who feels useless and unappreciated—you need to read this book. No matter who you are, if you struggle with situations, circumstances, relationships, or just plain negative feelings—you need to read this book.

Attitude-inize: 10 Secrets to a Positive You won't solve world hunger or save the polar bears or prevent meteors from crashing into the earth, but it will change your life from the inside out. And the next thing you know, people who meet you will find themselves wondering, *How can anyone be so happy and positive all the time? She must really lead a blessed life!*

When they ask you about it, do them a favor, will you? Hand them a copy of this book and encourage them to read it. Then watch them change, as the ten secrets to becoming a positive person take root deep within. They'll thank you for it. I promise.

Kathi Macias (<www.kathimacias.com>; <http://kathieasywritermacias
.blogspot.com>) is an award-winning author of more than thirty books, including the popular Extreme Devotion fiction series and her life-changing nonfiction book, *Beyond Me: Living a You-First Life in a Me-First World.*

INTRODUCTION

Tired of the "fast-food-new-attitude-to-go" mentality, promising instant gratification and a happy face without any real substance to back it up? Good—then you're reading the right book.

Attitude-inize: 10 Secrets to a Positive You is for everyday women—stay-at-home moms, women who work outside the home, college students, grandmothers, as well as married, divorced, and single women. If you're between the ages of twenty-one and ninety-nine and face discouragement in your daily life, you'll find within these pages concrete biblical solutions to help you create a new perspective that will have lasting results.

These secrets come just in time! Between foreclosure notices and layoffs, political rifts and global climate shifts, and personal and professional setbacks, we could all use a positive perspective adjustment right about now.

And more than ever, we need to understand the value of attitude. New research indicates that how you feel actually dictates how you do. More than skill, knowledge, or aptitude, your attitude dictates your performance and success. In fact, the Stanford Research Institute reports that only twelve and a half percent of a person's success in life is determined by knowledge; the other eighty-seven and a half percent comes from attitude.[1]

In other words, a healthy attitude is an incredibly valuable asset.

Build Your Positive Perspective from the Inside Out

"You're blessed when you get your inside world—your mind and heart—put right" (Matthew 5:8, TM).

The good news for anyone struggling to achieve and maintain a healthy perspective is this: change is possible, and it starts within. While many self-help books focus on the outer you, *Attitude-inize* provides the depth and truth necessary to equip you with a positive attitude from the inside out. In this book you will discover how to—

- Look forward to starting your day.
- Give more at work, home, and church—and get more out of it.
- Make a commitment to achieving your personal and professional goals.
- Rebound from defeat.
- Examine your heart and get rid of the negative junk inside.
- Quit depending on situations and people to make you happy.
- Transform from a victim mentality to a victorious, difference-maker attitude.
- Create and maintain a positive attitude—regardless of the outer circumstances.
- Change your perspective and discover how to see good in all things.
- Give and receive the gift of joy.
- Experience a new life!

Since 1989, I've presented workshops and keynotes to tens of thousands of people—funeral directors, chief executive officers, business owners, sales teams, administrative professionals, church leaders, women in ministry—motivating, encouraging, and equipping individuals to see good in their daily lives by adopting a positive perspective. The best part of my job is seeing women like you achieve actual results in their everyday lives—home, work, play, church—as a result of learning to positively manage challenging situations.

It's a process. That's why this book contains so many interactive, read-now-use-today activities to help you purposefully transform the negative to the positive. The tools to equip you—bite-sized applications, exercises, questions, action-filled stories, scripture, and inspiring wisdom—are an integral part of each chapter.

Ten Secrets

This book contains ten life-changing secrets for getting to the heart of a positive attitude. Consider these the ultimate in family values. Why do I say that? Because every woman has unique qualities, and when she becomes part of a family, those qualities amplify, becoming even stronger. Like the individual members of a family, these secrets work together to form a stronger, more positive you.

Here are the ten secrets:

1. Understand the power of attitude.
2. Respond rather than react to unexpected change.
3. Be accountable for your life.
4. Examine your heart *(kardia)*.
5. Forgive yourself and others.
6. Prepare for obstacles.
7. Learn to give and receive love.
8. Take charge of your thoughts.
9. Transform from the inside out.
10. Become a difference-maker in God's kingdom.

The bonus eleventh chapter, "Your Positivity Tool Kit," will reinforce what you've learned and help you sustain your progress.

The Ultimate Ripple Effect!

Like you, I have a past. In fact, I'm a lady who made more than my share of bad decisions and wrong choices. So rest assured that I've learned how to maneuver the waves and rise to the top with a new and improved perspective. In other words, as your guide, I'm experienced. In fact, I've survived tsunamis!

Don't worry about having to take this journey alone. I'll hold your hand, encourage you, and gently direct you. But I can do only so much, because cultivating a positive attitude begins with your decision and your decision alone. It's a commitment to a lifelong process of adjusting the way you think, act, and speak. But the reward will be a new, positive you!

Think of the ripple effect a positive perspective could produce in every aspect of your life. A positive perspective requires much more than simply seeing the glass as half full; it requires seeing the glass overflowing with grace, joy, and peace.

Imagine how that positive attitude could make you a better student, role model, church member, colleague, employer, mother, wife, sister, or friend. Remember—this is an investment in *you*. True change lasts forever, and the benefits of positivity never expire.

Here's to an exciting journey, filled with positive, healthy, from-the-heart attitude changes.

1 ✸ UNDERSTAND THE POWER OF ATTITUDE

Our attitudes control our lives.
—Tom Blandi

If you woke up this morning, shout, "Hallelujah! This is going to be one grand day!"

You're probably thinking *Wait until I have my coffee.* Nope, we need to keep the momentum rolling.

Remember the song "Don't Worry—Be Happy"? The lyrics to this cute song imply that regardless of life's circumstances, you can be happy. The problem? Even if you chant the lyrics fifty times, the words still lack substance. Have you ever tried saying, "Don't worry—be happy" during a Texas-sized emotional meltdown? How about during the height of a family disaster? The reality of this cliché is that women everywhere—from the boardroom, gym, church, and family dinner table—buy into the concept that they can just flash a big grin and magically reveal a positive, bubbly attitude.

Yeah, right.

Let's blame this superficial pop jargon on society. After all, the feel-good attitude yields instant gratification. But what else?

As a speaker, I often ask my audiences if they've ever attended a "rah-rah motivational-type" seminar. Nearly all the hands go up. Occasionally, the more rowdy participants even yell, "Yes!"

Then I ask, "Two days after that seminar, what concrete tools and principles are you still applying in your life?" Audience members typically scratch their heads and glance at the person next to them. Silence fills the conference room. Oops. From the podium, I can see the "rowdies" already wishing they hadn't shouted "Yes!" quite so loudly.

Why is motivation so fleeting? Stephen R. Covey, author of *7 Habits of Highly Effective People*, put it best when he said, "Motivation is a fire from within. If someone else tries to light that fire under you, chances are it will burn very briefly."[1]

Want to keep that fire burning longer? Try stoking it yourself next time.

Changing your perspective from negative to positive sounds simple, doesn't it? As a work-in-progress lady, I'm telling you that a positive attitude is certainly achievable, but it's not simple. It requires a lifelong commitment to change the way you view everyday experiences as well as the many challenging opportunities you may encounter. You also need a sincere desire to experience a "new you."

As I mentioned in the Introduction, I'm a woman with a past. My childhood lacked a positive, healthy atmosphere. I've made major bad decisions and wrong choices and lived with the consequences, including a stinky negative attitude for the first half of my life. Bitterness, anger, and envy hovered over me like a dark cloud.

During the second half of my life, God filled me with a desire and the power to transform and experience a new life. During this life-changing process, I've discovered the honest-to-goodness, power-filled benefits of a positive attitude from the inside out. And I'm not keeping them a secret. I want to share these secrets with you, because I want you to turn your pain, discouragement, and disappointment to positive passion as you discover and fine-tune your unique qualities—all of which help you truly realize a positive mental attitude.

The Value of Attitude

Did you know that your attitude is one of your most valuable personal assets? Perhaps you've never thought of it that way before. Few of us do. We've become so reliant on outside influences—mentors, experts, pundits, bosses, friends, family, teachers, support groups, the popular media—to the point we often *wrongly* believe attitude is something we're given or born with. Let me say this loud and clear: A positive attitude is not something that goes on *around* you; rather, it resides *within* you.

A positive attitude begins with a decision to get off the spectator bench and participate fully in order to develop and maintain a lifelong positive perspective. It requires self-discipline, practice, patience, and persistence. With that in mind, it's a good idea to discover why this commitment to a positive attitude is so valuable to you personally.

Chuck Swindoll, international speaker and best-selling author, writes,

Words can never adequately convey the incredible impact of our attitude toward life. The longer I live the more convinced I become that life is 10 percent what happens to us and 90 percent how we respond to it.

I believe the single most significant decision I can make on a day-to-day basis is my choice of attitude. It is more important than my past, my education, my bankroll, my successes or failures, fame or pain, what other people think of me or say about me, my circumstances, or my position. Attitude is that "single string" that keeps me going or cripples my progress. It alone fuels my fire or assaults my hope. When my attitudes are right, there's no barrier too high, no valley too deep, no dream too extreme, no challenge too great for me.[2]

During my motivational/inspirational presentations, I usually read Mr. Swindoll's poignant words to the audience, reiterating that life is ten percent what happens to you and ninety percent how you respond. I'm deeply moved when I observe audience members unfold their arms, lean forward in their chairs, and nod their heads in agreement. Some individuals even do a verbal "aha" or "hmm." Revelation? Inspiration? Motivation? Worth your investment of time?

Yes, your attitude is indeed one of your most valuable assets, and it's connected to your thoughts, deeds, and words.

The Heart and Soul of Your Attitude

Have you ever said something brilliant—or even stupid—and wondered where on earth those words came from? Want to hear something amazing? Your heart is connected to your mouth. The Bible clearly says, "The things that come out of the mouth come from the heart" (Matthew 15:18, TM). Thoughts and experiences stored in your heart come out of your mouth and directly impact your life and the lives of others.

As a speaker and writer, I love words. In order to better understand the real meaning of words, I have more than a dozen dictionaries (without dust) on my desktop. My favorite is *The Complete New Testament Word Study*, edited by Spiros Zodhiates. This hefty dictionary is an excellent tool designed to help readers properly understand the full meaning of God's Word (in the New Testament) as it was originally recorded in the Greek language. I often refer to this dictionary to help me grasp the depth and fullness of the Bible.

Case in point: the English word "heart" (from Matthew 15:18) translates to the Greek word *kardia*. Now you know where the word "cardiologist" originated. *Kardia* represents the heart as the soul— the focal point of human life. It denotes the heart, mind, body, and spirit as one, with the *kardia* (soul) as the controller.

In other words, *kardia* is the fountain seat of thoughts, passions, desires, appetites, affections, purposes, and endeavors. These components interrelate and produce—

- Positive or negative thoughts.
- Positive or negative words.
- Positive or negative actions.

This is great news. Now you can quit wondering, *Should I be negative or positive?* A positive, healthy attitude comes from within—your heart, mind, body, and spirit. It can't be bought. It can't be manufactured. You can't inject it, transfer it, or swallow it, because you already possess it. Positive change involves not merely inventing an optimistic perspective but discovering it deep within. Based on your willingness to be transparent and honestly look into your heart—and then doing something about what you discover—you can transform your attitude. The old adage "Is your cup half full or half empty?" reflects the relevance of a negative or positive attitude. It's all a matter of what you see.

Perspective

Want to enhance your life? Adjust your perspective. Author Katherine Mansfield writes, "Could we change our attitude, we should not only see life differently, but life itself would come to be different. Life would undergo a change of appearance because we ourselves had undergone a change of attitude."

Think about it: What if you weren't allowed to say, think, or do anything about a person or situation until you first caught them doing something right—or observed the incident from a positive perspective? Would this approach make a difference in what comes out of your mouth?

Carmen, a devoted mom raising three kids alone, grew tired of minimum wage jobs, living in near-poverty from paycheck to paycheck. Ten years ago she started a yard maintenance business. She worked long hours to earn enough money to support her children. She clipped coupons to save money on every item she purchased, including groceries, clothing, and household items. For years, Carmen and her children lived in a small, overcrowded apartment while she scrimped to save money in hopes of someday owning a home.

She finally bought that home. Sadly, within two weeks of moving in, she found that nothing about the house was worthy of positive mention. First, a slight crack in the concrete walkway destroyed her joy. Next, the front door didn't close properly. Later, water from the kitchen faucet dripped a couple of times. Carmen experienced what I call an "attitude-related meltdown." In other words, her reactions to new-home ownership needed adjustment. Plus, she made it a point to tell everyone she came in contact with every negative aspect about her house. All that arduous labor, all that scrimping and saving, and in less than a couple of weeks it seemed—to Carmen, at least—all for naught.

I don't know about you, but being an audience of one to a constant whiner is far worse than listening to a scratched music CD at warp speed—or mach ten! At least I can toss a CD into the trash.

By contrast, I have friends who live with painful chronic illness. These folks have real reason to complain—but they don't. This tells us two things: (1) maintaining positive attitudes in difficult situations is possible, and (2) sometimes complainers subconsciously are just waiting for someone to intervene by asking the right questions.

After several months of observing Carmen's negative attitude, I asked her if there were things about her home she liked. Her initial reaction was a bit haughty, but in her heart she knew I wasn't being sarcastic. I truly cared.

"Mrs. Coates," she replied, "are you thinking I don't appreciate my new house?"

"No, I believe you do. But don't you think you might feel better if you looked at the big picture, minimizing the negative and maximizing the positive aspects of your home that you worked so hard to get?"

Hesitantly, she nodded.

"Let's talk about the spacious kitchen. How do you like having room enough in the kitchen for the kids to cook beside you?"

"Oh, the kids and I like it. Last week we prepared meals for the hurricane evacuees and then delivered them."

"Well, how does it feel to have a family room big enough for you and the kids to read the Bible together as a family?"

"The room is cozy yet spacious, and it's perfect for us."

"How do the kids like having their own bedrooms?"

"They're delighted! Allie decorated her bedroom walls with her soccer ribbons, band awards, and a Bible verse poster. The kids finally feel a sense of home."

"Carmen," I explained, "over the years I've built several homes and lived in a couple of pre-owned homes. Minor adjustments to sinks, toilets, doors, and that sort of thing just go with owning a home. It takes a few months to work out all the minor issues; every homeowner is responsible for basic maintenance. Your Creator motivated you to work hard to purchase this home. When you display a critical attitude, how do you think God views the gifts He has given you?"

Her warm brown eyes filled with tears.

"I'm so ashamed. I need to be thankful, don't I?"

"Yes, my friend—you do. You also need to change your perspective regarding your dream home. Before criticizing your home, pause and envision the positive aspects so that negativity doesn't become your focus."

I noticed that my words penetrated her heart.

"Your life overflows with blessings. You enjoy good health. Your terrific kids are bright. You have a new home and a profitable business. By changing your attitude, you can alter your mood, influence the attitudes of your kids, and learn to cherish an attitude of gratitude."

Carmen smiled. "Thank you for caring enough to be honest with me. You're right—I need to count my blessings. Starting this very moment, I'm going to keep a mental checklist of the good things about my home and my life. I want to be a positive, appreciative example for my kids and others."

Several weeks later while I worked from my home office, I leaned toward the window facing the front yard and identified a buzzing noise. *Oh, no—another uninvited wasp family,* I thought.

I walked outside with my trusty wasp zapper spray can and stopped in my tracks. There Carmen stooped, her back toward me, weeding my purple pansies just below my office window, singing praise songs in Spanish. She turned around, flashed me a big grin, and embraced me with a Panda-size hug.

"Lovely music to my ears," I said.

"*Sí,* Mrs. Coates. I've replaced my complaining with a thankful heart and a joyful song."

And so it is with each of us, including me. As we change our attitudes, we see life differently, making life itself different. There is nothing more hopeful to me than knowing that with a slight attitude adjustment I can literally change the outcome of my day. Ask yourself: what could your day be like if you began it positively?

Aren't you finally ready to find out?

The Perfect Role Model

The *kardia* (or heart and soul) of Jesus Christ is the perfect role model for living life more positively. Ponder these words of wisdom:

1. Jesus faithfully prayed, continually seeking God's direction, and then He obeyed.
2. Jesus came to serve others, share the gospel, and lead an exemplary life.
3. People were not an interruption to Jesus—they were His purpose in life.
4. Jesus passionately loved people from all walks of life—prostitutes, beggars, thieves, no-account fishermen.
5. Jesus didn't find fault with people. He may have hated the sin, but He loved the sinner.

Jesus felt positively passionate about what He did and, equally important, who He did it for. If you follow Jesus' actions, deeds, and prayer life and mirror His love for humanity, your *kardia* will become fragrant and pleasing to God in accordance with His plans and purposes for your life.

I hope these words encourage you and fill you with a hunger and desire to be all God created you to be while embracing the importance of your "work-in-progress" attitude.

Oh, my friend, let your heart become pure and clean so you can truly experience change from the inside out! "As a face is reflected in water, so the heart reflects the person" (Proverbs 27:19, NLT).

Write your thoughts on what you've read.

_____

_____

_____

_____

_____

_____

_____

Questions

1. What kind of attitude did you wake up with this morning?

_____

_____

2. If you've tried to "don't worry—be happy," what were the results?

_____

_____

3. Can your attitude become one of your most valuable assets? If you think it can, explain why.

_____

_____

4. Please refer to Chuck Swindoll's attitude quote in this chapter. What is the single most significant decision you can make on a day-to-day basis? Why?

_____

_____

"When my attitudes are right, there's no barrier too high, no valley too deep, no dream too extreme, no challenge too great for me." How can accepting this attitude principle help you strengthen a positive focus on life?

_____

_____

5. *Kardia* represents the heart as the soul—the seat and center of human life. It denotes the heart, mind, body, and spirit as one, with the *kardia* (soul) as the controller. Are you ready to do some-

thing about your *kardia* in order to discover how to live with positive purpose? If yes, what actions come to mind?

_____

_____

6. How can your perspective affect your attitude?

_____

_____

7. Who is the perfect role model? Why?

_____

_____

8. "As a face is reflected in water, so the heart reflects the person" (Proverbs 27:19, NLT). How can this verse help you get to the heart of your attitude?

_____

_____

2 ✸ RESPOND RATHER THAN REACT TO UNEXPECTED CHANGE

When you respond to life, that's positive;
when you react to life, that's negative.
—Zig Ziglar

"Why aren't you living in a padded cell, babbling like a lunatic?" a Christian psychologist asked me after he listened to a portion of my testimony at a chapel service in New York. Even with all of his education and experience, he couldn't comprehend how I overcame my past traumas, losses, and pain to accept God's full-time ministry assignment to inspire, motivate, and encourage people from all walks of life.

We sat facing one another at a small metal table in the cafeteria. I wrapped my hands around my coffee mug and glanced into his kind eyes.

"A padded cell never occurred to me," I joked. "But, really, my surprisingly positive mental health is simple. I prayed for a new life, and God changed me."

The psychologist nodded, smiled, and encouraged me to keep telling my story about change in the hands of our sovereign Creator.

Change happens around us. It happens within us. If you live and breathe, change will be a big part of your daily life. Everything changes, except God. "I am the LORD, and I do not change" (Malachi 3:6, NLT). The rest of us? Well, change can be challenging and downright scary. But here's the secret to dealing with change: like our attitude, we can control how we respond.

Open the paper and read about something like a train wreck that kills twenty-five people because the engineer was suspected of text-messaging rather than paying attention to his job. You're disturbed. Those who died leave behind devastated and heartbroken family members and loved ones. Not a day goes by that the survivors don't grieve. Change? Yes, drastic to the extreme. As concerned citizens we feel compelled to think, *What a shame!* But, typically, that's the extent of our emotional involvement. Until tragedy hits us.

Certain changes come about by choice; other changes, like a train wreck, result from situations out of our control. Consider financial woes, marital problems, "no batteries required" toddlers, testy teens, the heartbreak of a prodigal son or daughter, college stress-out, illness, loneliness, depression, or the loss of a loved one. You're likely to find yourself somewhere in that lengthy—but by no means exhaustive—list. Whatever your situation, I'll gently guide you as we journey deeper into this thing called *change*.

Before we go any further, you need to know a couple of things about me. I'm a woman of my word, and I promise you no fluff. So, in order to dig beneath the surface, we need to establish an open line of communication. I vow to be authentic, vulnerable, and transparent with you. Will you do the same?

Good. Now let's examine the life-altering effects of change.

Learning About Change the Hard Way

My dad always said, "Jan, you can't always control situations or people, but you can control your attitude toward those situations and people."

I learned this the hard way.

Shh—Mama's still asleep. At age five, I stood on my tip-toes in the pantry, trying to reach the big jar of peanut butter and bread. Careful not to scratch the kitchen floor, I inched a chair to the counter to make a sandwich to eat while I walked to kindergarten. I thought I was being considerate. I even remembered to wash the messy knife. But apparently, in spite of my Herculean effort to stay quiet, I still woke my mother.

I heard feet stomping behind me. I turned and saw that Mom held a belt in her fist. "Why haven't you left yet?" She whipped my skinny legs. "Stupid—don't you know anything?"

Mom suffered from mental illness. I was her "evil child."

Dad hired housekeepers, cooks, and nannies, but they stayed for only short periods of time. Mom ran them off with her tirades and abusive behavior. More than once I watched from the stairway as Dad covered his face with his hands and wept while a medical attendant dragged Mom out of our home in a straightjacket. After a two- or three-month stay at the hospital, she returned home, and each time she seemed better, but only temporarily. Eventually I stopped telling Dad about Mom's physical, emotional, and verbal abuse, because I learned that every time I told, she ended up in the hospital.

I know Dad felt guilty. Me? I felt responsible.

Dad, a godly man, did his best to maintain normalcy in our chaotic lives. He owned his business and worked hard to support his family. He was a difference-maker who contributed to the greater good. His actions, words, and deeds taught me that I couldn't control many things in my life, but I should never give up.

Dad taught me by example. A humble, honorable man, he never admitted his deep, unshakable strength. But in my youthful eyes, he was like Samson, who ripped apart a lion with his bare hands. I remember sitting on his lap while he read me Bible stories. He took me to church and helped me memorize Scripture verses. When I was growing up, people frequently said, "Jan, you are your daddy." As a child and troubled young adult, I never understood those words; nearly fifty years later, I do. Today, *I am Dad*. He gave me his character, integrity, love of God, and strength never to give up, even when life seems out of control.

No child wants to be locked in closets, beaten with metal hangars, and cussed out for the millionth time. So to escape my private hell, I married young, thinking, *I'm just gonna leave this craziness and start a new life*. Shortly after my wedding, Dad divorced Mom.

Then, at nineteen I found myself divorced. The only good thing that came from that disastrous marriage was my son, Chris. While I typically avoid clichés, sometimes a meaningful one is so special it becomes emblazoned in our hearts. In this instance, the best way for me to describe my son is to say Chris became *the wind beneath my wings*. He taught me how to live, how to laugh, and how to love. Our closeness created oneness.

Talk about motivation! Chris's existence gave my life purpose. He was the reason I got up in the morning. He single-handedly gave me an identity—as loved mom, a real mother. His drawings and poems covered my bedroom walls. Chris crafted a cigar-box jewelry case for me one Mother's Day. In between multi-shaped red hearts, he wrote, "You are my happiness." Though I had no husband and Chris had no father, we had each another.

I worked full time, attended classes at a local university, and climbed the proverbial corporate ladder to financial and career success. Not long after, Chris and I bought a ranch and a couple of show horses that we showed together throughout the Midwest. We fished together. We went to movies, wrote songs, and hung out with my dad.

Sound perfect? It was anything but! Why? Because the attitude of my soul (*kardia*) was contaminated rot.

Chris spent every Saturday night with my dad while I "dated." Since Chris stayed over, Dad took him to a church in south Kansas City every Sunday. I had chosen a different path. In fact, by age fourteen I had quit talking to God. I decided He didn't want to hear from someone like me. After all, I smoked. I drank. I lied.

Dad would say, "Come on, Jan—spend the night here and go to church with us."

I just smiled and nodded, thinking, *Yep, sure thing. Just as soon as I make some changes and get my life cleaned up.*

I finally graduated from college as a thirty-something divorced mom. Shortly after, my office automation employer awarded me and other top sales representatives and managers throughout the country with a trip to the Bahamas, where I met and fell in love with a remarkable guy named Bill Coates. For the first time ever, Chris approved of a man in my life!

On July 30, 1982, Chris was the best man at our wedding. His teary eyes beamed with pride as he gave his "little momma" to another man. My nineteen-year-old son immediately appointed Bill as "Popsy," and we became a genuine family. Chris was happy, I was delighted, and Bill—the good-natured Mr. Wonderful—overflowed with joy. I thought, *Finally, a real family with abundant love!*

Unexpected Life Changes . . . Shattered Dreams

Red lights from a Missouri Highway Patrol car pulsed outside our remote country home in the early hours of October 24, 1982. A state trooper stood on our doorstep and extended something toward me.

"Is this your son's wallet, ma'am?" the trooper asked.

When I didn't answer, Trooper Marquart, who responded to my silent gesture and entered and stood on the ceramic tile foyer of my home, rephrased his question: "Ma'am, are you Chris's mother?"

I tried to speak, but my body shook, my lips quivered. Paralyzed words stuck in the bile-tasting lumps in my throat while my heart pounded so hard it felt as if it would jump right out of my chest. As danger alarms rang in my head, I didn't know whether to run, hide, or vomit.

Bill spoke up. "I'm Chris's step-dad, and Jan is his mother."

The officer nodded before speaking. "There's been a bad wreck, sir. I'm sorry, but your son didn't survive."

My legs buckled as the officer's words penetrated my denial. I felt my husband's strong arms catch me from behind as I cried, "No, God—not Chris!"

After the trooper left our home, I dropped to the floor and curled into a fetal position. With my head tucked in, knees tightly packed against my chest, I whispered, *Please, God—I need you! If you're there—*

I waited, begging God to reveal himself. In the quiet rage of my grief, He spoke the following words that changed my life: *Be still, my lost and broken child. Chris is with me. I love you!*

After nearly two decades of silence on my part, God not only heard me—He responded. I felt His warm strength encompass me. My body felt numb, weightless—as if a doctor had administered a massive dose of Novocain.

After what seemed like an eternity, Bill coaxed me to sit on the couch, where he just held me. My husband later told me he sensed I might take my life. Each time I journeyed to the bathroom to vomit, he followed me and stood outside the door. "Jan, are you okay?" he asked. In between my stomach heaves, we clutched one another.

And then, as we huddled together on the couch, the doorbell rang.

"Honey," Bill said softly, "Pastor Nelson is here."

"What? Who?" I sat up slowly. Then I remembered.

Roger Nelson was the minister of Lone Jack Baptist Church. Chris had broken and trained a couple of his Appaloosa colts.

Roger and Bill helped me to the kitchen table, where Roger held my trembling hands and prayed softly. "Dear God, help Bill and Jan during this tragic crisis. Encompass them with love and compassionate support."

By mid-afternoon neighbors and members of Roger's congregation—people I had never met—knocked on our door to express their sympathies. Some folks delivered baked hams, casseroles, and homemade pies. Others brought freshly picked flowers from their gardens and placed them on the lower steps of my front porch. Just before sundown, I glanced out the kitchen window toward the south barn and noticed two young men in my barn, feeding the horses and cleaning their stalls.

The kindness extended by those who didn't even know me stunned me. They came simply because they knew and loved my son. And they expected nothing in return.

Somehow we survived the next few days of Chris's funeral service and the out-of-town guests. Then our home went silent. I wandered around his room, touching his horse show trophies, saddle, and favorite boots. I clutched his pillow to my chest, smelling his scent, wishing the recent events were merely a bad dream.

Some days I couldn't get out of bed. I couldn't sleep or eat. The heaviness of depression consumed me. I felt abandoned at the bottom of a cold, dark well with no way to climb out. I watched the world and all its activity pass by in slow motion, my voice muted and my heart shattered.

I tried to pray, to talk to God, though words didn't come easily. At times I talked about my wonderful son. Sometimes I revealed my broken heart. Other times all I could do was groan and cry. Yet I continued to feel that God held me tenderly in His arms and listened to my sorrow.

Several weeks after Chris's funeral service, Pastor Roger came by our home again. Sitting between us at our kitchen table, he asked, "Would you folks allow me to pray for you?"

Bill and I looked at each other, nodded, and bowed our heads.

Father, you know the pain of losing a child, Roger prayed. *Your Son was killed, not by a careless driver but by men filled with hate and rage. God, only you can comfort Jan as she mourns the loss of her only child.*

As Roger prayed, I felt God's strength surround me, and for the first time I realized that God really did understand exactly what I was going through. He, too, had lost His only Son.

Several months later, shortly before Christmas, Bill and I felt strong enough to walk through the doors of Roger's church, the same church where, at the age of ten, Chris had been baptized. As we made our way up the aisle, people we didn't know walked up to us with hugs and kind words.

"I loved Chris, too," said an elderly lady.

"I miss Chris and pray for you every day," whispered a young boy.

"May we sit beside you today?" asked a middle-aged couple.

We were humbled by the kindness and love of this warm church family—these people who loved Chris and also loved God.

The service began with Roger's comments about the beautiful Christmas tree located next to the piano. "Some of you may have noticed our new Christmas tree in the front of the church. Our church purchased this reusable tree in honor and memory of Chris."

I glanced at the wooden cross on top of the tree and silently prayed, *God, thank you for helping us.* In that moment, the Lord reminded me of His love for me, assured His continued love and His comfort to me as I poured out my heart to Him about my son.

For several weeks, the only details we knew of the wreck were that Chris's truck had broken down and he had gotten a ride with a man driving a Camaro, which crashed, killing Chris, who was the only passenger. The driver walked away unharmed.

Later, the trooper would hand-deliver his written report to us. Two sentences stood out to me:

"Obviously drunk driver sped over 110 mph before losing control of the vehicle and flipping several times. DOA passenger was thrown 350 feet from scene of wreck."

In that moment, I felt a different kind of pain than I had ever experienced: helplessness—for my son who had innocently sought a ride home—and rage toward the driver. Out-of-control emotions consumed me.

Like many of you who are experiencing divorce, illness, loss of a loved one, financial distress, or job calamity, my life changed without notice and without my consent. Thankfully, Dad taught me that I couldn't control what happened but that I could control how I responded.

And so it is with you.

Even when life shatters into a million pieces, as it did when Chris flew through the window three hundred fifty feet to his death, hope reigns supreme. Naturally, Bill and I were shattered. When we removed the glass fragments that ripped the seams of our hearts, the wounds still existed. Yet we've found God's purpose in the midst of all the shattering. We've found beauty in the peace that passes understanding. God saves those jagged pieces of multi-colored glass and creates a thematic stained-glass rearview mirror of life—one for each of His human creations, including you and me. This illuminated artwork is often three-dimensional, representing how our pain and brokenness can be made into passion-filled good. But we cannot embrace our new life if we avoid change.

The Four Gifts of Change

The process of living through planned and unplanned changes, as well as making deep adjustments to our perspective, takes a lifetime. The unending adjustments require our patience as well as a willingness to receive the accompanying gifts.

As I journeyed through this tragedy, I found four gifts of change, all of which will enable anyone going through a crisis or unexpected event not only to survive the experience but also to rise above his or her situation. The question is—will you accept these gifts?

If your answer is yes, please pray the prayer below:

God, thank you for loving me so much that you freely give me gifts. Help me accept these four gifts with an open heart and an open mind. Steer me in the right direction so you can appropriate these gifts within me in a manner that pleases you. In Christ's name I pray. Amen.

These four gifts of change will help you learn how to respond rather than react to change with a new perspective.

- **Gift No. 1—Hope.** Committing to change gives you a vibrant, ebullient sense of hope. Hope stimulates you to seek positive purpose. Change is coming, it promises. Change can be made into good. Just the act of committing to change allows us to instantly feel more hopeful about not just the change we're going to accomplish but everything else in our lives as well.

- **Gift No. 2—Faith in God.** Real, lasting change—from the inside out—demands that we surrender ourselves to God's care. What a relief it is to quit trying to be in charge and let God— who created this world, the one who is sovereign and just, the one who loves you just as you are—make the decisions in your life! Place every ounce of your faith in God, because He can and will do the impossible. God is a deliverer, and He will see you through all things.

- **Gift No. 3—Clear Vision.** When we commit to change, we see our goal clearly and set definable actions for reaching it. Clarity offers such an uncompromising gift when it comes to turning pain to passion and experiencing a new life. When we see things clearly, we gain objectivity, which in turn allows us to be more appreciative and positive.
- **Gift No. 4—Energy.** Change can revive a broken heart or add passion to an otherwise routine life. Even the prospect of change can transform how we think, and that brings us one step closer to a more positive perspective.

Commitment to Change!

"*Change alone is eternal, perpetual, immortal.*" (Arthur Schopenhauer).

The *Kansas City Star* ran a feature article about Chris's death. Friends and strangers contacted me to express their condolences. I appreciated their letters, cards, flowers, and phone calls. I thanked them profusely, all the while feeling that none of them could relate to me. At least that's what I thought until Jean phoned.

"I'm Jean Jones from Hickman Mills, Missouri—I read about Chris's tragic death," she said.

"Thanks for calling." I waited for Jean to express her condolences. What I didn't know is that Jean had a life-changing gift waiting for me to accept.

"Jan, I know your pain," she said. "I lost my son and daughter-in-law six months ago to a drunk driver."

She did understand! Because she could relate to my pain, we connected. She then asked if Bill and I would join her and a couple of her friends for lunch.

Bill and I met Jean and her friends the following Saturday. We cried. We poured out our hearts. We joined forces with this group to found the Kansas City Chapter of MADD—Mothers Against Drunk Drivers.

I share this positive direction with you because in every life-changing situation, we have choices. In my circumstances at that time, I could have remained a victim and allowed my grief, anger, rage, and brokenness to keep me hostage. And eventually it would have destroyed me and everyone I came into contact with.

Believe me—starting MADD in my area was no cakewalk. Every time I spoke before senators, congressman, police officers, judges, students, and journalists I took a framed photo of Chris with me and placed it on the podium so others could see that my son was a real person. I spoke nearly every week for more than three years.

MADD saturated radio and television networks with its message and effected substantial change. Look how far we've come with regard to drinking and driving laws. Drinking while intoxicated (DWI) is illegal now. It's no longer a slap on the wrist to get behind the wheel of a car after consuming alcohol and causing a fatal accident. The laws are tough these days, but they weren't in 1982.

There is now a high public awareness of the dangers of drinking and driving. In addition, many schools support Students Against Drunk Driving (SADD). There are hundreds of MADD chapters across our great country. Why? Because people who faced devastating life changes decided enough was enough. Wounded individuals and concerned citizens refused to tolerate lenient laws, and they accepted the challenges associated with receiving the four gifts. They *hope* to make a difference, *embrace* their faith, *focus* on the positive vision of MADD, and *stay energized* to keep the momentum and passion alive. In other words, none of us loved the reason we started MADD, but we were passionate about making positive change a reality.

There will always be an empty hole in my heart because of Chris's needless death. But guess what—I'm no longer a victim.

Thankfully, I chose to accept the precious four gifts: hope, faith, clear vision, and energy. I live a life of victory, and so can you.

Marian Wright Edelman writes, "If you don't like the way the world is, you change it. You have an obligation to change it. You just do it one step at a time."

When Life Happens, Happen Back!

"The bricks have fallen down, But we will rebuild with hewn stones; The sycamores are cut down, But we will replace them with cedars" (Isaiah 9:10, NKJV).

Now that we've come full circle with our second secret, I have a quick question for you: How do you feel? Hope-filled? Encouraged? Motivated? Or do you still flounder in your grief and have a hard time accepting the gifts of change? That's okay. We all have our own timetables. Even so, this secret will help fuel you with encouragement. The good news about change is that it's contagious. The more you understand the power of change, the more you want to change.

Likewise, a positive attitude produces positive change. When I feel good, everything in life is better. Traffic doesn't seem so bad, work is more joyous, and I get more out of church. Even seemingly random moments—like lighting a candle at the end of a long day or baking a batch of cookies—take on new significance.

I can hint only so much at the benefits of positivity. It's truly like leading a horse to water. The horse still has to decide to take a drink. The true test will come as you begin to feel more and more positive yourself. Rest assured—change can and will happen. It's easy to doubt, to wonder, to worry, to fret. Many times this seems like our human default setting. Sadly, we tend to hear the voice of fear, distrust, and dashed dreams in our ears each morning as we rise to a new day. Life is hard and seems to be getting harder. Think how difficult it is to remain positive when bills pile up, credit cards max out, money is scarce.

On top of that, people disappoint us: acquaintances gossip, friends let us down, and even family members betray us. When even those closest to us seem distant and cold, we have a tendency to isolate ourselves. But the farther we retreat, the more we surround ourselves with woundedness, the less we can see God's light shining into, throughout, and onto our lives.

The fact is—bad things happen to us. How we *respond* is what we do to "happen back." The surest way to remain powerless, fearful, and negative is to let things happen to you without happening back. Let change be your ally in gaining a more positive attitude in life. Learn to embrace change to invite more positive emotions, wishes, and dreams.

I feel blessed to have you join me on this new life journey. Before we move forward, answer this question: can you remember a time in your life when you experienced deep, lasting inner change? If so, what happened before and after?

Exercise

If you have a brand-new spiral notebook, use it. If not, buy one. Or if you prefer, purchase a journal. Grab a label and a permanent marker. Place the label on the front of your notebook, and use your marker to write "Positive Journal." On the inside front cover write, "'I know the plans I have for you,' declares the LORD, 'plans to prosper you and not to harm you, plans to give you hope and a future'" (Jeremiah 29:11). On the first lined blank page and all subsequent pages, draw two vertical lines down the page from top to bottom. Label the first column "Date," the second column "Situation/Person," and the third column "Positive Change."

Pick a quiet time during the day or evening to faithfully devote five to ten minutes every day to write your experiences and thoughts. Each day before you begin your mini-journaling experience, reread Jeremiah 29:11. When you're ready to write, just do it! Try to record at least one thing you can identify as positive outcome so your notebook doesn't get lopsided. If after recording a negative experience you're unable to think of a positive change response, pencil in "pending."

Here's an example:

Date	Situation/Person	Positive Change
8-14	Bill's job situation is fragile at best. He's weary. I'm anxious, insecure, and getting on his nerves.	For today, I've— 1. Stopped playing career cop. 2. Focused on encouraging Bill. 3. Prayed for Bill while I walked three miles. 4. Reminded myself of Bill's professional talents and skills. 5. Created a marketing campaign for next year's speaking opportunities.
8-15	I hate physical exams. Today was the day—help! Impatience reared its ugly head. Two people slept in the waiting room. My initial reactions: 1. Reschedule exam. 2. Tap the "snoring" gentleman on the shoulder and ask him how long he's been waiting. 3. Remind Doc what a busy lady I am.	For today, I responded by— 1. Focusing on others. 2. Praying with Doc's assistant about her mother's death. 3. Not looking at my watch. 4. Thanking God for endurance to get through the ordeal and for good health.

Write your thoughts on what you've read.

Questions

1. When was the last time you experienced a positive change in your life?

---

2. If you could change one thing about your life right now, what would it be? Why?

---

3. I listed four gifts of change—hope, faith, vision, and energy. Dig deep and add a fifth gift to my list. What are the benefits of this fifth gift of change?

---

4. How are change and positivity alike? How are they different?

---

5. What if any valuable life lessons did you garner from my story about MADD?

_____

_____

6. "The bricks have fallen down, But we will rebuild with hewn stones; The sycamores are cut down, But we will replace them with cedars" (Isaiah 9:10, NKJV). How can this verse help you in getting to the heart of change?

_____

_____

3 ✹ BE ACCOUNTABLE FOR YOUR LIFE

Hold yourself responsible for a higher standard than anybody else expects of you. Never excuse yourself. Never pity yourself.

—Henry Ward Beecher

"It's not my fault."

"She made me do it."

"I forgot."

"I couldn't help it."

At one time or another we've all spoken these words. Blaming others is an easy rut to get into and a hard one to get out of. The truth of the matter is that we're all guilty of blaming others and creating excuses to justify our negative, less-than-desirable attitudes, which in turn manifest in our actions, deeds, and thoughts. When you blame others, you give up your power to get out of that negative trench and move toward a positive plateau.

Humans are creatures of habit. Blame others long enough, and it becomes habitual behavior. That's right: the blame game becomes more than a mere game—it becomes a habit, one that paralyzes positive progress and prevents you from experiencing a new you.

Want to know why I'm so familiar with this blame game? You've probably guessed. I lived with my own victim mentality for more years than I want to admit. Throughout my dysfunctional childhood and "colorful" young adulthood, I clung like a leech to the victim mentality, blaming others for everything—even my own wrong decisions and the related consequences—that didn't turn out the way I wanted. But God had other plans.

After Chris was killed by a drunk driver, I felt as if I had died too, leaving arms and legs and a blank face without a spirit. I didn't eat, sleep, or talk much.

But out of my only child's death, the holy sledgehammer of truth began to chip away at my "victim" heart. Miraculously, and over time, God resurrected me and transformed my hardened, broken heart to a soft, supple heart. Through the godly guidance of counselors, pastors, and friends, I discovered how to recall experiences of my past with an emphasis on good.

Someone once said, "Scars remind us where we've been—they don't have to dictate where we're going." This new mind-set is not acquired through a wish or a blink of the eyes. Rather, it's a process—one that begins with bold fortitude and a desire for real change.

Embrace Fresh Determination

"Replace your excuses with fresh determination" (Charles Swindoll).

Adjust the focus on your perspective, and you can discover how to view certain experiences from a different angle. Remember: it's not what happens to you—it's what you do with what happens.

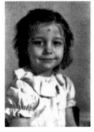 The photograph to the left is me at age seven. I remember this day as if it were yesterday. I woke up that morning and realized it was picture day at school. I glanced in the mirror and saw what I normally saw—a messy little girl with masses of tangled hair. I assessed the situation and summed it up with two choices: (1) I could ask Mom for help fixing my hair and risk causing an upheaval and perhaps not even making it to school, or (2) I could take matters into my own hands.

As you can probably tell from the photo, I chose the latter. With scissors in hand, I cut every single tangled mat from my hair as I whispered the song "Jesus Loves Me." I tossed handfuls of hair into the toilet and wiped my tears with the palms of my hands. I pulled my stained, yellow dress over my head, buttoned the back buttons, and marched out the front door to walk the three blocks to Horace Mann Grade School in Kansas City.

I walked through the open front door and noticed my class assembling in a room designated for school photos. I tried to blend in with the already organized line and stood with my arms glued to my sides in hopes that no one would notice my untidy appearance.

As I waited in line, pretending to be invisible, the photographer's assistant approached me. My legs shook. I felt the unwanted stares of my classmates. To avoid the glances, I focused my eyes on the tops of my shoes. Fear of being asked to leave the line shrouded me like a heavy cloak. The photographer's assistant stooped down toward my eye level. She gently placed her hands under my chin and tenderly lifted my head so that our eyes made contact. Her lower jaw dropped at least six inches. She then exhaled deeply with a hushed sigh.

"Sweetie," she whispered, "I'll be right back."

"Sweetie," she had said—not "loser," not "stupid," not even "ugly."

The fear within me eased. I was safe. I stayed in line.

True to her promise, the photographer's assistant returned to me within a few seconds with her purse in hand. She carefully placed her purse on the table next to me and opened it. She reached in, pulled out a comb, and began the massive task of trying to fix the mess atop my head.

She thoughtfully combed my ragged hair. This kind woman moistened her fingers with her tongue and began to caress my hair, placing a hair pin on the right side of my head to keep the "loose ends" in place.

She then placed her hands on my cheeks and whispered, "Ah—much better. You look very nice."

As a wounded seven-year-old child, I probably didn't even thank this kindhearted lady. There amidst my peers, already feeling conspicuous, I may have felt too self-conscious to share my true feelings of gratitude and relief. But today I loudly, proudly say, "Thank you from the bottom of my heart for making me feel special."

This lady's kindness and compassion made a positive deposit within my *kardia*—my heart, body, soul, spirit, and mind—a deposit filled with God's love.

I could look back on my childhood and focus on the many negative experiences and trauma. Believe me—they would fill several dumpsters. But I choose to zoom in with my God-powered positive lenses while holding dear the treasures that help me maintain a positive focus. Memories that accumulate healthy interest help me reflect in the rearview mirror of life and see God's goodness.

God promises us that "Every detail in our lives of love for God is worked into something good" (Romans 8:28, TM). Something good abides there—I promise you. Yes, even beyond the pain and scars of the past reside sprinkles of light and dashes of hope. Have you ever looked through a kaleidoscope? If so, you know the multicolored shapes can produce magnificent images. The viewer looks into one end, and light enters the other end, reflecting the rainbow of colors via a tube of mirrors. If the viewer fails to hold the kaleidoscope to light, it doesn't work properly. Think of it this way: God is the light in our lives. In His perfect timing, He appropriates the exact amount of light into the kaleidoscope of our souls, changing the shattered, harmful images into a perfect picture of His goodness one image at a time.

That's why I keep the light-filled memories of the photographer's assistant in the forefront of my mind. This radiant, goodness-filled image reminds me that indeed God can make good from all things. By focusing on the positive, I replace my bad-attitude excuses with fresh determination to press onward and upward. I choose to fill my thought life with positive deposits so I have a reserve balance during times of emotional drought. And so can you.

Your thought life is the very place to begin a positive perspective revival—one without excuses, one without blaming others. The quality of your thought life determines the outcome of your day, the outcome of your week, the outcome of your life here on earth.

Tommy Newberry, author of *The 4:8 Principle*, writes, "No area of your life is untouched by your thoughts. Your habitual thinking patterns either encourage you toward excellence or nudge you into weakness."[1]

Only one person can determine what thoughts you dwell on: you.

In order to be all God created you to be, let the words of the apostle Paul saturate your soul:

Summing it all up, friends, I'd say you'll do best by filling your minds and meditating on things true, noble, reputable, authentic, compelling, gracious—the best, not the worst; the beautiful, not the ugly; things to praise, not things to curse. Put into practice what you learned from me, what you heard and saw and realized. Do that, and God, who makes everything work together, will work you into his most excellent harmonies (*Philippians 4:8-9, TM*).

As I said before, when we walk through the narrow gate of redemption and salvation, we realize it's not what happens to us—it's what we do with what happens.

Our problems may have started with the mistakes and wrong-doings of others, but we often compound these problems with our bad decisions.

Let me say this plain and simple: What other people have done to you does not define who you are. What has happened in your life—job loss, divorce, a wayward child, the loss of innocence, illness, disappointment, the death of a loved one—is not punishment. Your past is not cause for you to accept a victim label or live a life continually blaming others and making excuses for the difficulties you face. Blaming does not improve your overall well-being. Rather, blame actually gets in the way of experiencing a positive perspective. Blame causes you to limp through life taking one step forward and two steps back.

Blaming others only hinders you from learning accountability and responsibility for your own life. Besides that, blaming others continues to give those others power and control in your life, making you a victim. The power to change resides in the power to quit blaming others.

Here's the real truth: God doesn't want excuses. He doesn't want you to blame others for the way you live your life or the way you face each new day. Remove that sticky, ugly "victim" label. Choose to persevere. Eagerly embrace God's redemption and salvation interlaced with the promise of a new beginning each and every moment of the day.

No one has immunity from life's challenges, nor is anyone guaranteed a perfect life without difficulties. However, you are *not* left alone to deal with every blow that comes your way. God promises to rescue you while filling you with hope, perseverance and the strength to soar through each day. God's Word promises, "The righteous person faces many troubles, but the LORD comes to the rescue each time" (Psalm 34:19, NLT).

With your eyes focused on Jesus, you can quit blaming others and embrace a fresh perspective.

Avoid Self-pity

"Self-pity is our worst enemy, and if we yield to it, we can never do anything wise in this world" (Helen Keller).

Emily, the mother of three beautiful kids and wife to a wonderful husband who dearly loved her and provided quite well for the family, consumed her life with self-pity. When I met Emily, I was working one full-time job and one part-time job and attending a community college two nights a week.

Early one Saturday morning, Emily phoned me.

"Wanna pick me up this morning so we can shop?" she asked.

Sure, I would like to hang out with her, but how? When? My mind raced as I glanced at the pile of dirty clothes sitting in the living room. Shop? Who will go to the Laundromat for me? I have a three-page to-do list, a minimum of four hours of homework, and I'm in desperate need of rest.

"Sorry—I've got a packed day," I responded.

"No one has time for me. The kids are fighting. John is working again today. Why me?"

I begged forgiveness and promised I would try to make time the following Saturday. As I picked up the pile of dirty clothes scattered on the floor, I thought about how Emily's "Why me?" thing was actually becoming her persona.

Occasionally on a sleepless night, my mind wandered to a private place where I would envision my imaginary future husband kissing me good night and whispering, "I love you"—three words John literally lavished on Emily. John, a model dad and husband, demonstrated his love for her with flowers, date nights, and helping out around the house. But for whatever reasons, Emily couldn't muster contentment or happiness. In her mind, everyone seemed to have it better than she did.

Don't get me wrong: there's a difference between feeling sorry for yourself—which is a temporary frame of mind—and perpetual self-pity. We're all guilty of having occasional pity parties for which the door prize may include realizing just how good we have it after all. And sometimes a good cry cleanses the soul, providing a catharsis that makes us feel even better afterward. But when we wear self-pity as a badge connected to our identity, it's time to stop and assess the situation.

I've listed below three disciplines to help you avoid self-pity:

Don't seek or expect sympathy. Everyone knows the story of the boy who cried wolf; don't be the person who continually cries sympathy. Most people are kindhearted to real issues that merit their time, prayer, and action. But if you're a whiner who frequents self-pity on a regular basis, even the most patient and sympathetic people will avoid you. Rather than seeking empathy, practice extending compassion to someone less fortunate than you.

Don't compare yourself to others. When you notice the achievements of others, don't give in to envy—it eventually leads to self-pity. Instead, ask yourself what the person did to accomplish his or her achievement. Analyze the person's strategy. If it's a good one, emulate it. Focus on your God-given gifts, your talents, your strengths. Take a look at your weaknesses, and make goals to improve them.

Help others. Some people who seek self-pity are so tuned in to their own issues that they forget others may have more serious problems. A good way to get out of the self-centered pity mode is to walk out your front door, and as you close the door behind you, make a mental note to leave your problems behind. Then focus on helping the less fortunate. Don't believe me? Check with anyone who has served a Thanksgiving meal at a homeless mission. Or ask a devoted hospital volunteer about the rewards of helping others. Notice the smiles on the faces of Salvation Army bell-ringers.

Practice Self-control

Learning to hold yourself accountable requires self-discipline in all aspects of your life. Like everything that is worthwhile, making self-control a habitual behavior takes practice. When you catch yourself reverting back to negative blame-game behaviors or pity parties, hit the "stop" button of your mind. Take a break, and fill your soul with a positive environment. For example:

- Turn on your stereo and listen to praise music.
- Read uplifting Bible verses and quotes.
- Surround yourself with upbeat people.
- Make entries in your journal that highlight nice deeds others have done for you.
- Make a list of your blessings, outlining all the things you are thankful for. Include the clothes on your back, your family, your friends, the food you digested earlier today, the roof over your head. In other words, count every blessing.
- Take a walk outside. Close your eyes for a few moments, and then blink them open while pretending to see God's creations for the very first time. Reflect on the wonder of that butterfly or freshly sprouted blade of grass.
- Stand up, take a deep breath, and purposefully inhale positive thoughts. Then exhale negative excuses.
- Thank God for creating the unique, special, work-in-progress you.
- Voice a prayer for someone else.
- Make a written list of your positive, special memories from your childhood.
- Thank God for allowing you to wake up this morning.

These simple suggestions can help you stay disciplined and help you discover how to be accountable for your attitude. As you become more proficient at filling your soul with fresh determination, minimizing your pity parties, transforming the negative into positive, and not blaming others, you'll add to this list and creatively customize it to suit your needs.

One last thought: the next moment is a new beginning. How do you want to begin it?

Write your thoughts on what you've read.

_____

_____

_____

_____

_____

_____

Questions

1. Have you ever blamed someone else for something that happened in your life? If so, describe how this action hurt you more than the accused.

_____

_____

2. "It's not what happens to you—it's what you do with what happens." How can this revelation help you adjust your accountability attitude?

_____

_____

3. Say this verse out loud: "The righteous person faces many troubles, but the LORD comes to the rescue each time" (Psalm 34:19, NLT). How do you feel knowing God promises to rescue you?

_____

_____

4. Blaming others continues to give them power and control in your life. How can knowing this help you remove the "victim" label?

_____

_____

5. As you grasp the importance of personal accountability for your life, what actions can you take to reach this goal?

_____

_____

4 ❀ EXAMINE YOUR HEART

Search me, O God, and know my heart.
—Psalm 139:23, NKJV

Everyone holds onto unhealthy thoughts from time to time. Whether they're a result of unkind words spoken by a friend or family member, rejection, or personal failure, damaging thoughts have a tendency to linger. Some store these experiences in an "instant recall" area. They tell everyone within listening distance about their hurts. Others let their hurts fester without their conscious consent. This unhealthy garbage prevents us from experiencing a lifelong positive perspective.

That's why it's so important for you to commit to a permanent healthy soul. Unfortunately, it's not a one-time decision or an occasional glance into your soul. Rather, a fit heart is a result of timely, routine examinations that search deep below the surface.

When was the last time you had an in-depth physical examination?

The American Medical Association recommends that every healthy person thirty-five and over pay a yearly visit to the doctor for a comprehensive physical examination.

After the patient checks in and completes the necessary paperwork, a nurse or physician's assistant leads him or her to the examination room. Once there, the patient sheds several layers of clothing and sits nearly naked on the examination table, covered by a starched gown with four tie-strings dangling on the front side.

The examining physician uses a basic stethoscope to help determine the health of the patient's heart. While the stethoscope provides physicians and nurses with a tool to measure irregular heart rhythms, it is limited in what it can detect.

A standard stethoscope cannot detect attitude. It cannot determine if you're depressed or elated, hopeless or hopeful. It cannot analyze the condition of your spiritual heart, mind, body, and soul (*kardia*), nor can it detect irregularities that interfere with your overall spiritual health and well-being.

The health of your *kardia* is rather a personal matter—so personal, in fact, that secrets, past traumas, disappointments, fears, and anxieties remain buried deep within the crevices of your heart, so deep that you may not know they exist. The good news is that God knows everything about you. He knows the number of hairs on your head (Luke 12:7). He knew you before creation (Jeremiah 1:5). He knows your pain and sorrow as well as your healthy and unhealthy life perspectives. God loves you unconditionally regardless of your past or present.

A physician administers care to patients by appointment only. But you don't need an appointment to spend time with the Great Physician. He's available 24/7—no appointment necessary. In order for God to use His spiritual stethoscope, you simply come as you are with an attitude of spiritual nakedness. By being completely vulnerable and transparent, you present yourself ready and willing to reveal your soul to God. Please remember: this exercise is not for God—it's for *you*. Why? Because when it comes to your spiritual health, you don't have an objective viewpoint. You may not even notice those pesky culprits directly responsible for that negative perspective.

Search Your Soul

"The LORD's light penetrates the human spirit, exposing every hidden motive" (Proverbs 20:27, NLT).

When I speak about searching your soul, I engage audiences by using a toy red and blue plastic stethoscope. I encourage attendees to raise both hands in the air so I can get a good reading of their attitudes. They giggle but eagerly raise their hands. I place the ear pieces in my ears and position the scope in the air toward the audience and declare my findings, which usually include—

- Stress
- Fear
- Lack of contentment
- Anger
- Sadness
- Elusive happiness

I sometimes ask, "Is anyone stuck—unable to move on?" as I grab my trusty plunger. Some ladies eagerly nod affirmation; others glance down and avoid eye contract with me. "It's okay," I say. "I've been there. It's nothing to be ashamed of. Plus, you know what they say about admitting you have a problem. So—"

I pause and wait for them to look back up at me. "Are you ready to get rid of the negativity in your lives?"

The audience yells a resounding, "Yes!"

I then pray aloud, asking God to search the hearts of every attendee and reveal the garbage that needs to be released to Him. This simple prayer acts a bit like the release form you sign at your physician's office. By praying, you ask God to search your soul; you give Him permission to show you what His spiritual stethoscope reveals.

Now, reader, I must ask you three questions:

Are you ready to change the way you think?

Are you willing to adjust the manner in which you respond to situations?

Will you let God search your heart so you can grow from the inside out?

If you answered yes to these three questions, I encourage you to pray the following prayer.

God, I open my heart to you. Search the depths of my soul. Show me my fears, doubts, wrongdoings, and inappropriate thoughts. Show me what you already know and see. Make it plain and simple so I can work with you to release the negativity in my life. In Jesus' name I pray. Amen.

One of my primary problems was that I didn't give God access to my heart. I see the former contents of my *kardia* clearly today, but thirty years ago I was blind to my true inner spiritual health. As I said previously, self-objectivity is difficult. In fact, if God had placed His spiritual stethoscope on my heart, He would have found six primary heart defects:

Resentment

Jealousy

Hardness of heart

Anger

Low self-esteem

Bitterness

Not a pretty picture. Sure, some of the toxic contents within my heart were directly related to my dysfunctional childhood, what other people said about me, as well as the effect of sins committed against me. On the other hand, I bore the guilt of poor decisions, wrong choices, my lifestyle, and allowing the actions of others to contaminate my *kardia*. In other words, I owned my unhealthy attitude. You can do the same thing. Positive or negative, you own your attitude.

Not sure how to accomplish this feat? Here are three simple ways to *own* your attitude, one letter at a time:

O—Out with the bad. Give God your bad, negative, unclean thoughts. This practical decision requires more than just sweet talk or happy thoughts; you must choose every day to see the light instead of the dark, the good instead of the bad, the hope instead of the hopelessness. I know it's hard. God knows it's hard. But no one can make these choices except you.

W—Win every time. Everything in life is a win/win, even your most challenging troubles. It goes back to the old adage that God closes a door and opens a window. Didn't get that new promotion? Lost your job? Guess what—now more than ever the time is ripe for "accidental entrepreneurs" to give in to their dreams and follow their passions. When you experience a closed door in your life, remember to open your eyes and look for God's grace-filled window complete with unexpected blessings.

N—Never give up. This journey requires stamina and commitment. When you're tempted to turn around and return to the "old" you or even quit, press on toward the goal while seeking God's light. How many times have you started something only to quit when the going gets too tough, the investment doesn't pay off as you expected, or the pounds aren't shed fast enough? Failures can bring us down. But remember: there is no failure in simply trying and not giving up. Remember how far you've come. It will help you create positive choices—and therefore a positive attitude—each and every day.

I must admit that change within my heart has been a long, gradual process. Part of my daily routine includes allowing God to search my heart and remove any and all negative attitudes from my soul. During particularly challenging seasons of life, I often seek God's spiritual stethoscope on an hourly basis.

Here's the truth: God wants every part of you to be negative-free. He desires to fill your soul to the brim with love. God longs for you to create and maintain a lifelong positive perspective. Always remember that God loves you just as you are, but He loves you too much to leave the negative junk in your soul. Don't be shy or embarrassed by what God might find in your soul "for He knows the secrets of every heart" (Psalm 44:21, NLT).

Take a few moments to pray. Ask God to search your heart. Give Him full access to your entire soul. This exercise offers a major turning point in becoming a new you.

Will you commit to being a cooperative patient as the Great Physician continues to examine your soul?

Recognize Core Issues

I, God, search the heart and examine the mind. I get to the heart of the human. I get to the root of things. I treat them as they really are, not as they pretend to be *(Jeremiah 17:9, TM)*.

Years ago I worked with Haley, a lady whose husband abandoned her for another woman. Sadly, her marriage ended in divorce. The experience broke Haley's heart—it totally devastated her. The raw, excruciating pain left her as fragile as a shattered teacup carelessly glued together with aged, chalky, white paste. Like other rejected wives, Haley's sense of being was fractured. Her damaged self-worth deposited a toxic trail, undetectable to the human eye or a medical doctor's stethoscope.

Being a divorced mom, I could relate to Haley's grief. I wanted so much to befriend her, to offer her wisdom and insight. I thought perhaps that since I had walked a similar journey, I might help steady the many crooked roads of self-doubt and hopeless deadends she would face.

One morning I surprised Haley with a single crimson rosebud. I hand-delivered the rose to her as she sipped her cup of black coffee in the corporate break room.

"Good morning, Haley," I said. "I brought you a rose to remind you that you're special."

She broke down in sobs and said, "Thank you, Jan. No one knows how I feel."

"You're right; I really don't know how you feel. But I've been a divorced mom for quite some time, and I've discovered that the pain of rejection and abandonment eases with each passing day."

"You're lucky—you have a child," she said.

"That's true. Chris gives me the motivation to get out of bed every morning. He loves me unconditionally."

"I'm totally alone. No one finds me attractive—not even me." Haley clutched her cup with both hands. "What man in his right mind would be interested in someone like me?"

"Listen—you're an attractive, intelligent young lady. You have a lot to offer in a relationship."

"I'm afraid if I allow myself to get into another relationship, the same thing will happen: another sexy woman will destroy it."

"Haley, the attitude of your heart is filled with negativity. You're judging every man by the actions of your ex-husband. How long have you been divorced?"

"Seven years."

"Seriously? Seven years? What does your ex-husband's life look like today?"

"He moved on. He married the woman who ruined my marriage. They have three young children and live in a nice home." Haley stared at her hands in her lap.

"Hmm. While I believe he has made some bad decisions, he has settled down and created a new life complete with a family. But you're still living in the past. Seven years is a long time to grieve a divorce."

"You don't understand. I can't get over it." She fidgeted with the silver-toned watch on her left wrist.

"Getting on with your life is a decision—one that you personally choose. May I encourage you to find new interests, get involved in a singles group, and start experiencing some form of fun in your life? Only you can decide whether to live your life as you are now—continually holding on to every negative thing that has ever happened or boldly changing the attitude of your heart by doing something positive from this day forward."

Haley picked up the rosebud and placed it up against her chest. She stood up, thanked me for the rose, and headed down the hallway toward her office. She seemed distant yet deep in thought.

You've probably known someone like Haley, or perhaps portions of her story hit home. Sometimes it's hard to bounce back and press on when life seems bleak and unfair. That's why it's important that you understand some of the root causes of negativity that God clearly sees with His spiritual stethoscope. These include—

- Low self-esteem
- Stress
- Fear
- Resentment and anger
- Inability to manage change

Because everyone experiences these emotions at one time or another, we can't really blame the emotions themselves. Instead, being unable or unwilling to get rid of these emotions can lead to a bad attitude. Interestingly, Haley's negativity mirrored my attitude of thirty years ago.

Now that you've read a portion of Haley's story, maybe you can relate to her circumstances. Maybe someone has wronged you. Or perhaps you're in a position to encourage a coworker or a friend. Whatever the case, take note of the core issues, because they are consistent. In other words, regardless of the cause, the effect is similar.

When we come to terms with core negativity issues, we can learn to put the past behind us and face the present with a clearer focus interlaced with a positive perspective. Ralph Waldo Emerson wrote, "Write it on your heart that every day is the best day in the year."

Always remember: enhancing your attitude awareness enables you to experience a change of heart. Isn't that what this adventure is all about?

Experience a Change of Heart

"You never know how or when God might sober them up with a change of heart and a turning to the truth" (2 Timothy 2:25, TM).

As a sales manager for a major computer company, I spent eighty percent of my time flying from one city to another for face-to-face meetings with prospective and existing clients. When I had a day in the office, I spent it either on the phone or in meetings. Several weeks had passed since I had given Haley her rose and offered her my objective input. Back in the office to get caught up on paperwork, I stopped by her office.

I tapped on her open office door. With her phone cradled against her shoulder, she nodded me in and motioned me to a chair located across from her desk. I sat. After hanging up the phone, she glanced my way and smiled.

Wow! Haley can smile—and what a pretty smile at that!

"So how you doing, pretty lady?" I asked.

"Good," she said. "You won't believe this, but I actually took some of your encouraging words to heart."

"I'm so proud of you. Tell me about it." Inside, my heart melted for her.

"Well, I asked a couple of my friends about singles groups for divorced people. Then I went to my first meeting, which was held at a Presbyterian church just a few blocks from my apartment. I met so many nice people and realized I'm not really alone. I must not be ugly, because several nice guys introduced themselves to me and encouraged me to keep coming to the meetings. One guy even said something about an upcoming dance and asked me if I would save him a dance."

Just like the red rosebud I gave to Haley, she began to blossom over time. Haley's transformation began with a decision to change her heart. The closer she drew to God, the more her heart healed. The more her heart healed, the more her perspective changed from negative to positive.

By joining this support group, Haley placed herself in a safe environment to share the contents of her heart with God and others. You can imagine God winking and lovingly saying, *That's my girl! Show me your wounds, sweet Haley. Now we're making progress. My daughter, you will experience newness of heart.*

Later Haley joined that Presbyterian church—a church that opened its doors to the brokenhearted. How like God to nudge His Church body to reach out to a wounded woman and fill her heart with love, acceptance, and hope!

The Great Physician is always right beside you. He cheers you on through that trial or the hurts inflicted by someone's actions. He stands ready, willing, and able to search your heart and help you let go of the past and press forward to the future with a positive, healthy perspective.

The apostle Paul clearly outlines one of the Great Physician's prescriptions for your attitudes and actions:

Brothers, I do not consider myself yet to have taken hold of it. But one thing I do: Forgetting what is behind and straining toward what is ahead, I press on toward the goal to win the prize for which God has called me heavenward in Christ Jesus *(Philippians 3:13-14)*.

Allowing God complete access to your soul, identifying and recognizing attitudinal core issues, and letting God transform you from the inside out are steps you need to practice the rest of your life. Don't demand perfection—just keep looking forward to the present and the future.

In the next chapter you will gain a better understanding of what forgiveness is and how it affects your attitude.

Write your thoughts on what you've read.

_____

_____

_____

_____

Questions

1. How does it feel when you combine your new positive perspective with God-filled passionate energy?

_____

_____

2. What is the difference between a physician's stethoscope and God's spiritual stethoscope?

_____

_____

3. If God searched your soul today, what would He find?

_____

_____

4. Ask God to help you "O.W.N." your attitude. Fill in the blanks next to the three steps below:

1. **O**—Out with the bad.	A. Describe your negative, unclean thoughts that get in the way of positive accountability. _____ _____
2. **W**—Win every time.	A. What doors have recently closed in your life? _____ B. Close your eyes. Blink several times, and ask God to open your eyes to His grace-filled windows. Write down what you see. _____ _____
3. **N**—Never give up.	A. What are you experiencing in your life that requires total commitment and prayer to press on? _____ _____ _____

5. Ralph Waldo Emerson wrote, "Write it on your heart that every day is the best day in the year." What actions can you take to make Emerson's words a reality in your life?

_____

_____

6. In Philippians 3:13 Paul writes of the importance of "Forgetting what is behind and straining toward what is ahead." This

is God's desire for you. Read the prayer below, and complete the blanks:

Dear God, I want to have a positive perspective and be accountable for my life. Help me forget _____

_____

_____ .

Put it behind me so I can press forward to what you have in store for my grace-filled future. Prepare my heart for learning to deal with forgiveness. In Christ's name I pray. Amen.

5 ✹ FORGIVE YOURSELF AND OTHERS

Forgiveness is not an occasional act; it is a permanent attitude.
—Martin Luther King Jr.

I shivered and glanced toward the sky where brilliant sun rays trickled through the partly cloudy, late-afternoon skies. The yellow-and-white crocus that adorned the south meadow of our twenty-acre Missouri ranch danced in rhythm with the gentle breeze. These delicate flowers that beacon the coming of spring beautifully illustrated the reality of my hope—a promise for newness of life, a transformation from dormant to vibrant. *Thank you, Lord,* I whispered.

It was Easter Sunday 1983, just six months after we had buried our only son, Chris. My husband, Bill, held my right hand while we walked from the parking lot to the church. My left hand gripped our small overnight bag that contained two white robes, two towels, and two outfits. We walked into the designated room, removed our coats, shoes, and socks, slipped our robes over our heads, and sat on the gray metal chairs, waiting for Pastor Roger Nelson. I crossed and uncrossed my shaking legs several times. I inhaled and exhaled deeply in an effort to calm the pounding within my heart.

Pastor Roger peeked in the room, saying. "Are you guys ready?" Bill and I nodded and followed him to the baptismal pool located about twenty feet behind the wooden pulpit. This was a second baptism for both Bill and me, and it represented a renewal of our vows with Jesus, a rededication of our lives to Him after years of walking our own walk.

I glanced at members of our church family who were in the pews. Several people wiped tears from their eyes while others sat silently with their heads bowed.

Pastor Roger baptized Bill first and then glanced in my direction while extending his gentle hands. I was immersed in the crystal clear baptismal waters that shimmered with light and life—the same baptismal in which Chris publicly witnessed to his receiving of Jesus Christ as his Lord and Savior at the age of ten. I felt a special closeness to my son there—a closeness I yearned to keep.

At the same time, I experienced the holy presence of Jesus. My white robe floated in the water as if angels were lifting the hem of my garment toward heaven. Going into the baptismal represented a burial of my old life; coming out was a resurrection. I nestled back in Jesus' arms with a new spiritual cleanness. I was a woman restored in the name of the Father, the Son, and the Holy Spirit.

My relationship with Jesus had been transformed from dormancy to a life filled with hope, and I treasured my renewed relationship with Him. In His eyes I was sparkling clean; my sins were washed away. But there existed a stark contrast in the way Jesus regarded me and how I viewed myself. Like a warped DVD, my mind repeatedly replayed bad scenes from my life. I was certain about my eternal future, but the guilt from my past filled my conscience with a desperation that attempted to choke life out of me.

"Yes, but—I've got a past." Every time I heard someone speak about God's grace and forgiveness, those very words echoed in my mind. Hey—I'm not your perfect Christian lady, sitting on the third row, center pew of the church. I'm a lady who's made more than my share of wrong decisions and bad choices. Bottom line: I could have been condemned and stoned two thousand years ago by the religious legalists of Jesus' day. That's right—I was a sinner, but now I've been saved by His grace.

Embrace Truth

Most of us find it extremely difficult to be objective about our personal shortcomings, our wrongdoings, our sins. But remember our promise early on in this book? We pledged gut-wrenching truthfulness as well as vulnerability and transparency with one another. I admitted to the sin I've committed. What about you? Have you ever intentionally lied? Have you told tiny fibs? Have you occasionally withheld portions of truth to make your words seem innocent and free of trickery? Have you experienced feelings of pride, envy, or self-righteousness? Or at the opposite end of the spectrum, have you ever done something so bad that you think you've blown it completely?

First, if you answered yes to any of these questions, I want to thank you for being honest. Whether they are great or small—from murder to fibs—we all have sin issues we've had to deal with. It's just a matter of identifying them and admitting the truth about them. Second, welcome to the world of fallen people, a family that includes you and me. Every human being, even a child, knows the sting of sin.

"This one's a gift," said the local grocery store owner years ago as he handed me a candy bar. "Remember, young lady—next time you must pay for it." Embarrassed and guilt-ridden, I vowed from that day on that I would quit stealing. A rebellious teen, I lied to my high school teachers about homework projects I never completed. I forged notes from home to cover my frequent absences. More than once my dad grounded me for months for abusing his weekend curfew rules. My out-of-control behavior escalated. I blossomed into adulthood as a self-made woman—independent, strong-willed, self-centered—who tried to numb her pain with alcohol, cigarettes, and the wrong kind of love. Some might explain my behavior as typical of a victim of childhood abuse in which sexual promiscuity, anger, self-destructiveness, and aggression are considered "acting up." Others would say I was a wounded, mixed-up person. Whatever the core issues of my past, I'm a big girl now, and I must own my actions as well as any resulting consequences.

Let's pause to cover the topic of sin. What is sin? Sin is mentioned hundreds of times in the Bible, starting with the "original" sin when Adam and Eve ate fruit from the tree of knowledge. The Bible tells us that sin is

- An offense against God (Psalm 51:4).
- A failure to reach God's perfect standard (Romans 3:23).
- A failure to obey God's law (1 John 3:4).
- A failure to do the good we know we should do (James 4:17).

We've all fallen short. On our own, we can't climb out of our muddy sin trenches, no matter how hard we try. We need someone to rescue us from the mire. We need an advocate who will present our case.

So God provided the Savior. He does offer forgiveness for sin. This is truth, but it is often hard to accept.

As I look back over my life, it is clear that I wanted to change. I wanted to be a better person. I wanted to put my past transgressions behind me. But I didn't have the ability to forgive myself, because I wasn't spiritually equipped to measure the impact of my sins. At that time in my life, I didn't understand the importance of forgiveness. I didn't comprehend that my unforgiveness of self and others actually prevented me from moving beyond my old issues. Looking back, I realize my unforgiving spirit got in the way of everything positive in my life.

My journey has taught me that until we accept God's forgiveness for our wrong thoughts, actions, and words, and forgive those who have hurt us, we are walking with one foot nailed to the floor and the other running in a circle. It's a futile exercise filled with negative ramifications. Without the right kind of forgiveness in our lives, positive attitude changes that we've made thus far will disintegrate without notice.

Abundant grace and forgiveness form the basis of a healthy heart, mind, body, and soul (*kardia*). Oswald Chambers wrote, "Forgiveness is the divine miracle of grace."[1] Grace-filled forgiveness can improve your mental and physical well-being. This special forgiveness is important because it—

- Releases resentment.
- Reduces stress.
- Enhances your peace of mind.
- Increases your life expectancy.
- Clears your conscience.

And there's more! Accepting God's forgiveness of your sins and extending that same forgiveness to others helps you move beyond the past and propel yourself into the present—and the future—with radiant, godly positivity.

Many people have said, "Forgiving others is easy—it's forgiving *me* that I have a problem with." That's probably true for most of us with the exception of abuse and criminal offenses committed against us. Forgiving myself and accepting God's forgiveness for my sins was a major process for me. I stumbled. I failed. But the sweetness of grace tenderly wrapped with loving forgiveness relentlessly lured me. I knew about the gift, but I didn't understand how to receive it.

Much like grace, gifts represent a transfer of something without need for compensation. When a friend remembers your birthday with a gift, what do you do with the gift? More than likely, you thank your friend and open the gift. Unfortunately, we often leave God's precious gifts unopened, because unresolved guilt whispers, "Yes—but I'm ashamed of the choices I made in my past."

No sin disqualifies us from receiving God's forgiveness. The Bible makes it plain that prostitutes, murderers, liars, thieves, adulterers, and cheats all received God's grace-filled forgiveness gifts. That means our idle gossip, the pride we experience when others applaud our good deeds, our food indulgences, and our pangs of jealousy toward the tall, slender coworker who seems to have it all together qualify us for needing God's grace. Like our biblical ancestors, our past becomes ancient history when we receive and open God's gifts of forgiveness and grace.

Accept God's Gift of Forgiveness

"By grace you have been saved through faith, and that not of yourselves; it is the gift of God" (Ephesians 2:8, NKJV).

On that Easter Sunday when Bill and I rededicated our lives to Christ, Pastor Roger and the special church family at Lone Jack (Missouri) Baptist Church celebrated with us by serving generous portions of prayer, cookies, and fruit punch immediately after the service.

They loved on us and helped us cope with the overwhelming grief of losing Chris. In the midst of our pain, they gave us godly examples to follow. They didn't preach at us or thump on their Bibles. They opened their arms to embrace us—just as we were, brokenness and all. These godly people baked casseroles and pies for us. They brought us fresh-cut flowers from their gardens. Their thoughtful actions and warm embraces saturated our home with the fragrance of lovingkindness while filling our hearts with much-needed love. Through this incredible "family," we personally experienced Jesus' love. We broke bread with our new family. We participated in clothing and food drives for the less fortunate. We joined small group activities and began reading our Bibles.

For several years we listened intently to sermons explaining God's unconditional love, His promises of eternal life in heaven, and a future filled with a new beginning. Like many believers, listening to sermons was easy; applying the messages to our lives took some doing.

One Sunday Pastor Roger preached about God's gifts of grace and forgiveness. "You don't need to live your life walking around consumed with guilt, because God has great and glorious gifts for you," he said.

I readjusted my sitting position. I crossed my legs. I folded my arms. I wiggled in my seat some more. But the words "consumed with guilt" seeped into every seam of my heart. I glanced up toward the pulpit. Yep, he was looking right at me.

Over the past couple of years, Pastor Roger and his wife, Mary Jane, had befriended Bill and me. I enjoyed our fellowship, keeping my past pretty-much a secret. But listening to him that morning, I knew without a doubt that Pastor Roger was speaking to me. Did he know about my party-girl past? Did he know I used to smoke and drink? Did he know I envied the mom with three kids sitting on the pew directly in front of me? My arms and legs failed to barricade my heart from my shame.

"When you confess your sins to Jesus and repent, your sins will be forgiven," Pastor Roger continued. "Accept God's gift made possible by Jesus Christ today."

Tears streaked my face as God used guilt, shame, and remorse to get my attention. I was a woman convicted of my need to accept God's gift of forgiveness. *Yes, Lord—I accept your gift,* I prayed silently.

I was tired of constantly tucking away my dirty little secrets. I grew weary of my past getting in the way of my future. I was frustrated that my positive perspective constantly wilted without warning because of my past actions and thoughts. In other words, subconsciously I craved a change.

How about you? Are you ready to take the next step? If you are, please pray the following prayer:

Lord, I'm ready to make my past transgressions history by fully accepting your grace-filled gift of forgiveness. Show me how you view my past. Show me my half-truths as well as my pangs of jealously and pride. Convict me of my wrong attitudes and actions. Help me experience real repentance. In Jesus' name I pray. Amen.

Accepting God's forgiveness gift is not a one-time decision—it is a lifelong commitment. It's a daily, sometimes hourly, process in which we surrender our past attitudes and mistakes while embracing what I call "life-restoring CPR." This simple acrostic represents three easy-to-remember words.

C is for Confession: Acknowledge your wrongdoings, and confess them to God.

P is for Prayer: Seek God's presence through prayer, and have a heart-to-heart talk with Him about your past.

R is for Repentance: Feel sorrow for your wrongs. Repentance means remorse with a change of direction.

This kind of CPR can remove the guilt you've been harboring while bringing about personal renewal, spiritual revival, and that new, positive perspective you've longed for.

Experience Personal CPR

"If we confess our sins, he is faithful and just and will forgive us our sins and purify us from all unrighteousness" (1 John 1:9).

The exercise of confessing our sins, praying, and repenting guides us into a lifestyle that cultivates godliness and removes habits that lead us into sin. When we follow this process, Scripture demonstrates that not only will God forgive our sins, but also our intimate relationship with Him is restored. The CPR process is between you and God. It requires sincerity and action.

Beginning this process can be difficult for most of us. We may begin CPR with past issues that easily come to mind. I encourage you to tackle sins with a one-thing-at-a-time mentality. If you try to take on twenty years of past sins, you'll get overwhelmed and frustrated. Rest assured—God will bring to mind your sins in accordance with His plans and purposes and in His perfect timing. He knows when and if we are ready to address tough issues, as well as how to orchestrate this CPR process.

I've outlined the CPR steps to help you get started.

Confession: Write your wrongs. God promises to give us a clean heart, but first we have to come clean with Him. We may begin CPR by setting aside a quiet time to reflect and recount our wrongdoings. Open your heart and mind to God, and let Him reveal what you need to see. It's helpful to write down what God reveals to you about your life, because it forces you to be specific. If you simply grasp a concept with broad ramifications by saying, *God, I really messed up my life,* you miss the opportunity to acknowledge and confess the sin issues God wants you to deal with. During my long and painful confession process, I jotted down my sins on the pages of a spiral notebook, I wrote journals, and I wrote notes and letters to God. The important thing to remember is to write your wrongs and then pray.

Prayer: Have a heart-to-heart talk with God. In the presence of God, you are safe and secure. God will never betray you, nor will He repeat to others what you've shared with Him. Look at it this way: God already knows the details of every single sin in your life; He's just waiting for you to confess them to Him. So when you pray, pour out your heart, confess your sins one by one—don't hold back. The rewards of a clear conscience and a clean heart await you just on the other side of your confession prayer. Just think: no more secrets, no more fear, no more guilt-related anxiety. After you confess your sins to God, ask Him to forgive you, and then accept His forgiveness. Hold God's grace tightly with all your soul and all your might. Jesus is speaking to you and me when He says, "Your sins are forgiven. . . . Your faith has saved you; go in peace" (Luke 7:48, 50).

Hint: Don't be surprised if Satan keeps reminding you of your sins even after you have confessed them to God and fully accepted His grace-filled gift of forgiveness. When this happens, remind yourself that God has forgiven you and that your past is wiped clean. Then tell Satan to get out of your life, and mean it.

Repentance: Make a 180-degree turn. Repentance does not mean asking the Lord for forgiveness with the intent to sin again. Repentance means that we acknowledge our sins, regret our sins, and commit to change. Through confession, prayer, and repentance we experience forgiveness—the Holy Spirit begins to conform us to the image of Jesus. We become saints who will be made perfect in our eternal life.

Oswald Chambers says, "Strictly speaking, a person cannot repent when he chooses—repentance is a gift of God. The old Puritans used to pray for 'the gift of tears.' If you ever cease to understand the value of repentance, you allow yourself to remain in sin."[2]

I've actively pursued CPR for more than twenty-five years. When I first accepted God's grace and forgiveness, I was unaware of the depth of sin that had wormed its way into my soul. The CPR process created excruciating pain in my heart that felt as if the Holy Spirit were squeezing the truth out of me ounce by ounce. As images of individuals I had hurt through lies and deceit came to mind, I wrote them down. One by one, I confessed my sins to the Lord, and with each new confession the pressure on my heart lightened. I remembered people from long ago with a clear picture of the anguish I caused. I remembered my party-girl life with extreme guilt. Like the old Puritans who prayed for the gift of repentant tears, God blessed me with the gift of warm tears that softened my hardened heart.

It took months of guidance and conviction from the Holy Spirit for me to complete this process. When I completed this portion of my repentant confession, I vowed never to let my sins build into mountain-size again. From this painful lesson I learned the importance of confession, prayer, and repentance for my sins at least daily and sometimes hourly. For all of us, commitment to CPR is a lifelong process. Our job is to listen to God by reading the Bible and to live with an open, transparent heart while basking in His grace.

God offers immediate and freely given forgiveness. Our transformation from a person guilty of wrongdoings to a forgiven person takes only an instant. When King David prayed, "Generous in love—God, give grace! Huge in mercy—wipe out my bad record. Scrub away my guilt, soak out my sins in your laundry" (Psalm 51:1-2, TM), God immediately forgave his sins. And so it is with us. Our sins are washed away and we are made clean and whole. Like our biblical ancestors, when we accept God's forgiveness, we experience a new life complete with a new beginning.

We also experience a need to extend that same forgiveness to those who have sinned against us.

Release Your Burdens

"Cast your cares [burdens] on the LORD and he will sustain you" (Psalm 55:22).

I began to feel a little self-righteous after my massive confession, prayer, and repentance process, until the Holy Spirit reminded me through sermons, Bible study, and wise mentors of my need to release and forgive others.

I knew I needed to release my anger and hurt to God in order to mature as a Christian and move forward in my new life journey. After much soul-searching, I fell to my knees and asked Jesus to help me recall the sins committed against me, to guide and direct me toward complete forgiveness of others. As He revealed these sins to me, I knew I needed once again to grab a spiral notebook to record my hurts.

* * *

*Resentment is like drinking poison and
then hoping it will kill you enemies.*
—Nelson Mandela, winner of the Nobel Peace Prize

* * *

Throughout the next few months, God continued to divulge my hurts that had been caused by the sins of others. The names and sins flowed from my pen with ease. It felt good to finally acknowledge the pain that had festered into toxic anger and bitterness. It felt even better to pray and release these burdens to God. Now He owned them, not me. I later placed the nearly full notebook into the fireplace and burned it. I felt as though one ton of toxic waste had been removed from my heart. Mind you—these hurts were not criminal offenses or abuses committed against me. These sins were serious but not life-threatening. For example: a longtime friend forgot my name after Chris was killed; a former boyfriend broke my heart when he dumped me for another woman; a cruel boss tried to bully me.

Many months later the Lord woke me early in the morning. I got onto my knees and began to pray. In my mind, I heard the Lord say, *Jan, let's finish releasing the sins committed against you that still burden your heart.*

Shocked, I thought the Lord had me confused with someone else. I whispered, *Lord, no. I've already released and forgiven everything. Look at me—I'm a new person.*

No, Jan, I have waited patiently. You still have huge burdens in your heart. Come—surrender them to me. Let go.

Father, believe me—we've done this, I pleaded.

The Lord continued, *But Jan, you need to release the rage at the man who killed Chris. Your immense pain is poisoning you. Give it to me. Let go of the anger caused by relatives who sexually abused you. Jan, release your mother for the physical and emotional abuse you endured as child. My precious princess, your rage and anger will destroy you.*

Well, this time I thought the Lord had gone too far. He had asked way too much from me. After all, how could I release my anger about such vicious crimes? Besides, none of the individuals involved were remotely remorseful. They had never uttered a simple "I'm sorry."

Lord, I can't do this, I sobbed.

I can. Surrender it all. I want every burden in your heart released so you can feel the fullness of my love.

Several hours later I prayed for release from my rage and resentment.

During this long and painful prayer meeting with the Lord, I sobbed until I could hardly catch my breath. Finally I let go and surrendered.

✳ ✳ ✳

When a deep injury is done to us,
we never recover until we forgive.
—Alan Paton

✳ ✳ ✳

I awoke the next morning and noticed the radiant sunlight beaming through my bedroom window. Though exhausted after such a long struggle with God, I felt like a new person. I was free! It's important to note that I didn't pardon the man who killed Chris. I didn't pardon my childhood abusers, nor did I excuse their behavior. I did, however, allow the Lord access to my heart by releasing their wrongdoings to Him and relinquishing my claim to retaliate.

God calls us to let go, to release the sins committed against us to Him. That's the process we're commanded to follow. Over time we will experience real forgiveness toward those who have sinned against us. As children of God, He permeates us with the same power that raised Christ from the dead. God's power enables us to forgive others with the very same grace and forgiveness that you have received from the Lord for your sins.

Taking Steps to Forgive

As we learn to accept the Lord's forgiveness for our own sins, we can finally extend that same grace to those who have sinned against us. The Bible says, "You must make allowance for each other's faults, and forgive anyone who offends you. Remember, the Lord forgave you, so you must forgive others" (Colossians 3:13, NLT).

Through faith and obedience you can begin to see God's hope-filled promises materialize. God will make forgiveness a reality as you take the following steps.

1. Ask God to reveal the unforgiveness in your heart.
2. Acknowledge the sins committed against you.
3. Acknowledge the pain, bitterness, and resentment.
4. Surrender the unforgiveness to God.

Following is a sample prayer:

Father God, I confess that ____(name of person)____ hurt me when he [she] ____(name of offense)____. It made me feel (rejected, unloved, unable to trust, and so on).

Father, you have said that all things are possible through Christ Jesus. I claim this promise and ask that you release my anger against ____(name of person)____.

Through the power of Christ Jesus, I surrender the sin and the pain to you. Help me experience true forgiveness, Lord, right now through this prayer.

In Jesus' name. Amen.

Remember—we do this for ourselves. Holding on to wounds caused by another person hurts only us. The other person is probably merrily going about life. We need to do the same thing while embracing God's abundant grace.

Choose to Forgive

This process of forgiving self and others is an important part of your journey. Whether it's a minor offense or a major offense, don't take this forgiveness process lightly. It's for your own emotional and physical well-being, for both short-term and long-term. Hang in there with diligent perseverance. Press on—the rewards are worth it!

Say this with me: "I choose to forgive!"

Choose forgiveness this day—this very moment. God's supernatural power will enable you to remove every burden from your heart in order to experience a new, positive perspective from the inside out while allowing you to truly be set free from your past.

Write your thoughts on what you've read.

_____

_____

_____

_____

Questions

1. Many believers struggle with sin issues. Describe how you've fallen short of reaching God's perfect standard:

_____

_____

2. God's grace-filled forgiveness can improve your mental and physical well-being. This special forgiveness helps you release feelings of resentment, reduce stress, enhance peace of mind, increase your life expectancy, and clear your conscience. Accepting and extending that same forgiveness to others helps you move beyond the past and propel yourself into the present with radiant positivity—ready to live a new life. How can this truth personally help you?

_____

_____

3. What happens to your past when you receive God's gift of forgiveness and grace?

_____

_____

4. In the "Accept God's Gift of Forgiveness" section I wrote that I experienced Jesus' love through our newfound church family. Describe how you've experienced the love of Jesus through other believers:

_____

_____

5. Confession, Prayer, Repentance (CPR) can remove the guilt you've been harboring. What else can you experience?

_____

_____

6. **Confession: Write your wrongs.** Practice this exercise by writing God a note: *Dear God, I acknowledge that I sinned when I*

_____

_____

7. **Prayer: Have a heart-to-heart talk with God.** In the presence of God you are safe and secure. God already knows the details of every single sin in your life. He's just waiting for you to talk to Him about them. Write a short prayer: *God, I come before you ready for change. I know you know everything about me and love me unconditionally. I just want to talk about*

_____

_____

8. **Repentance: Make a 180-degree turn.** How is the Holy Spirit conforming you to the image of Jesus?

_____

_____

"You must make allowance for each other's faults, and forgive anyone who offends you. Remember, the Lord forgave you, so you must forgive others" (Colossians 3:13, NLT). Pray about this Scripture, and describe how it speaks to you.

_____

_____

6 ✹ PREPARE FOR OBSTACLES

Stand up to your obstacles and do something about them. You will find that they haven't half the strength you think they have.
—Norman Vincent Peale

"You've lost your identity," the counselor said. "You're no longer a mother."

I sat in the counselor's office identifying and extracting remnants of jagged pieces of glass that ripped every seam from my heart caused by the drunk driver who killed Chris. Though I initially sought counseling every other week, I had reached the point, after nearly two years of grief therapy, at which I went only as needed. My massive grief interfered with my thinking ability. Remembering names and details challenged me. I found it daunting to focus on conversations and recall the context. But my counselor's words "You're no longer a mother" felt like a fire-hot electrical jolt that seared those five words onto my heart. I trembled. I sobbed. I sunk deeper into the tan leather couch and emotionally disengaged myself from my counselor. He got up from his chair, paced a few steps, then sat on the edge of his desk, just two feet from me.

"Listen to me," he urged. "You have so much love to give. You and Bill are still young. You need to think about starting another family."

I heard him!

Before leaving his office, I promised to speak with Bill about the possibilities of rebuilding our family. I prayed the entire forty-minute drive home. *God, if starting anew is part of your plan for Bill and me, guide and direct us. Make room in our hearts for a family. Help us make it happen.* Over dinner, I told Bill about my counselor's advice. He smiled, gently squeezed my hand, and said, "Honey, I've been thinking the same thing. We can never replace Chris, but we can add to our family and be great parents to our future children."

We agreed to launch our journey with physical exams. Our family physician gave us clean bills of health, saying, "You two are healthy enough to raise ten kids, but don't wait five years to get started." Because we were nearing forty, he sent us to several fertility experts, where we discovered that past health issues prevented us from conceiving a child. In other words, we failed the fertility tests.

Our positive hope for a "new family" was shattered. Our childlike glee hushed. Even our orange cat, Morris, slept somberly at the foot of our bed rather than on his pillow between our chests. Bill dove into his work in an effort to fill the void. Me? I managed to function at work even though a dark cloud of discouragement hovered over me.

As you read this, perhaps you can relate to the discouragement and fear that strained my perspective. Regardless of the cause—job uncertainties, stressed relationships, health problems—discouragement and fear create havoc with our attitudes. Obstacles surround us. They challenge even the purest of optimists. Billy Graham said, "The Christian life is not a constant high. I have my moments of deep discouragement. I have to go to God in prayer with tears in my eyes and say, 'O God, forgive me,' or 'Help me.'"[1]

Like Billy Graham, we lay our tear-filled requests at the altar. We beg God to help us persevere. We plead rescue from the black pit of discouragement.

From the depths of my despair, in between sobs, I prayed, *Why did you get my hopes up about children? Oh, God—help me!*

Seek Godly Counsel

After several months of grieving our infertility issues, I phoned my counselor.

"You're a strong, determined woman, Jan," he said. "When God closes one door, keep knocking. There are two things I want you to do. First, I want you and Bill to pray about adopting children. Second, read Isaiah 41:10."

That evening, I snuggled in my warm blanket with my Bible in hand. I obediently opened it to Isaiah 41:10—"Don't be afraid, for I am with you. Don't be discouraged, for I am your God. I will strengthen you and help you. I will hold you up with my victorious right hand" (NLT).

I read and reread this verse. I personalized it by writing my name in the margin of my Bible and read it again. I read it out loud to Bill. Later Bill and I prayed. By the time we said, "Amen," God had filled us with the courage to reopen the sacred, ever-so-fragile areas of our hearts to His plans to grow our family. We met with our pastor, who wholeheartedly encouraged us to pursue the adoption process. We talked to friends at church who had successfully adopted children. We attended adoption forum meetings sponsored by local government agencies. We prayed some more.

I can't stress enough the importance of godly counsel, especially when discouragement and fear cloud sound thinking. Godly counsel includes talking and praying with your pastor, meeting with a trusted counselor, reading your Bible, listening to the advice of wise friends and family, and personally talking with God. The Bible says, "Without good direction, people lose their way; the more wise counsel you follow, the better your chances" (Proverbs 11:14, TM).

Godly counsel helps us get past fear and discouragement. It clears our cluttered thinking and helps us move beyond tunnel vision to objective vision. The wisdom of godly people spurs us to spiritual and emotional clarity while helping us get rid of our fears, anxieties, problems, and discouragement. The key is to listen and be willing to change, to move forward instead of backward. Living a healthy life with a positive perspective requires that we obtain godly counsel on a regular basis.

Take heart. God declares that He will strengthen and help us. He promises to hold us up when we're too weary to hold ourselves up or when we just need a gentle hand to help us balance our walk. God is all-powerful. He spoke the world into existence—imagine what His victorious right hand can do in your life. It's your turn to personalize Isaiah 41:10 by placing your name in the blank spaces.

God created me, ____(your name)____, and He is with me. I won't be discouraged, for God is my God. God will strengthen me and help me. God will hold me up with His victorious right hand.

God will see you through every circumstance. How does that make you feel? I hope you feel encouraged and ready to move forward in your adventure.

Pray Big

Looking back, I admit my prayer life sometimes sounded more like whining sessions in which I constantly begged God, *Please give me a new chapter in my life.* I omitted specifics and failed to acknowledge His sovereign power. Did I pray too small?

Most parents teach their children to pray small, easy-to-remember prayers like "God is great. God is good. Let us thank Him for our food." Praying small is a natural childlike response that teaches kids to honor God Almighty with thankfulness.

The problem is that we tend to revert back to small prayers. We need to grasp the greatness of who God is. As adults, we need to pray in awe of God's desire to bless us with His provisions, to unveil

His plans and purposes for us. When we want something extraordinary done, we need to emulate individuals who know firsthand that God responds by exceeding all expectations.

Case in point: George Fredrick Mueller (1805-1898), a Christian evangelist and director of orphanages in Bristol, England, cared for more than 10,000 orphans during his life. He had a passion for sharing God's love with children under his care while also providing them with an education.

Through all this, Mr. Mueller never made public any requests for financial support, nor did he go into debt. Rather, he prayed specifically, one-by-one, for each need—financial assistance to pay off the orphanage shelters as well as food and clothing for the children.

Many times unsolicited food donations arrived at his doorsteps only hours before the children needed to eat, further strengthening his faith in God. Every morning after breakfast, he read his Bible and prayed. Mr. Mueller made sure each child received a Bible upon leaving the orphanage. His ministry stirred a deep compassion for orphans in England. Fifty years after Mr. Mueller began his work, more than 100,000 orphans had received care in England alone. He did all this while preaching three times a week from 1830 to 1898.

A godly man? Indeed! It is said that Mr. Mueller read the entire Bible more than 200 times. After much Bible meditation, he prayed specifically for each need.[2]

We can learn from Mr. Mueller's Bible study and prayer example. God's Word is filled with deep wisdom that can help us learn how to pray big simply by personalizing and rephrasing. The following are examples to help you practice this process.

Scripture

"If we hope for what we do not see, with perseverance we wait eagerly for it" (Romans 8:25, NASB).

Sample Prayer

Refresh my hope, Lord. Help me aim high like a majestic eagle. Let me never say, "I quit." Fill me with the power to hang tough in all circumstances. Teach me determined perseverance. In Jesus' name I pray. Amen

Scripture

"I can do all things through Christ who strengthens me" (Philippians 4:13, NKJV).

Sample Prayer

Invigorate me, Jesus. Fill me with the stamina to focus on you rather than dwell on challenges before me. Together we can overcome all obstacles. In your name I pray. Amen

Scripture

"With man this is impossible, but not with God; all things are possible with God" (Mark 10:27).

Sample Prayer

Almighty God, you are all powerful and infinitely able to do all things. Teach me to believe every word in the Bible. Show me how to pray specifically for each need. Help me pray big. In Christ's name I pray. Amen.

Now that you've read a couple of examples of praying scripture, try it.

Scripture

"I focus on this one thing: Forgetting the past and looking forward to what lies ahead" (Philippians 3:13, NLT).

Satan hate woman true because woman gave
life. Satan is to destroy life. Reclaim life.
hold on. Faithful in those prayers.

Stay focused. Practice patience. Be ready
We are not in charge. God is

Pg 99. Do I want God's will be done, or
be told by God OK, have it your way.

Phil 3:13. New start, Jesus chose to walk
through life with God as God. Forget what I've
been through, all the roots, and the backward
days. Stand anew.

Some of the Obstacles that come our
way are hidden inside us

Ps. 37:3,4 Trust in God do good have safe pasture
Delight self in the Lord, discover desires
of our heart & receive.

Obstacle - job change, circumstances,
trusting too much too little; health, Finances,
family relationships

pg 89
In my life hurting God?
God is moving away the mountains; Do I
need to weather experience. Just want
for God here. Feels like staying in the
same place
1. Seek godly counsel Is 41:10
He does it through other people
Talk to friends about it. Also - The Bible Personal
verse
Pray big. God I do believe, help my disbelief.
Be humble enough, vulnerable, that we are
struggling, our hearts are't ready yet
What matters - what God prepared for us or what
others say about you. When we meet obstacles,
don't shrink dreams, pray big. Get close to
accomplishing dreams, more obstacles

Write a practice prayer based on Philippians 3:13:

_____

_____

_____

George Mueller's can-do, positive perspective, based on the truth of God, allowed him to passionately pursue and experience God's will for his life. His faithful walk with God illustrates the relevance of obeying God's will. Mr. Mueller didn't initiate Internet, e-mail, or direct mail campaigns in an effort to generate donations. He didn't make television or radio appearances to plead for funds. He simply prayed.

You, too, can personally experience God's amazing plans for your life by praying big. God doesn't want us to pray generically for a new chapter in our life, as I so often did. Rather, He desires us to focus on Him and pray specific, big prayers while He writes a new book for our lives.

Stay Focused

"You did what?" Bill asked. His bright blue eyes twinkled with delight.

"I mailed more than fifty letters to adoption agencies," I said.

As a sales manager for a Fortune 500 computer company during the 1980s, I had access to technology and databases. My secretary, on her own time, helped me launch this massive project. When the last envelope slid out of the printer, I placed the personalized letters and envelopes in my car.

While Bill made business calls in another state, I sat at my kitchen table, humming praise songs and praying silently. One by one, I signed the letters and licked the stamps. The next day I hand-delivered my sealed hopes and prayers to the post office. I knew Bill would be pleased.

"Well, Honey, you sure know how to propel things from neutral to overdrive," Bill said, flashing a warm grin.

The truth of the matter is that God energized me. He filled me with strength and determination. Countless people prayed specifically for God to open adoption doors for us. Our adoption attitude transformed from timid inaction to a courageous campaign.

Sometimes just being faced with a difficult decision is polarizing. We make excuses. We get distracted. We need strength and direction. The Bible, our life compass, encourages us with just the right words: "Then you'll get where you're going; then you'll succeed. Haven't I commanded you? Strength! Courage! Don't be timid; don't get discouraged. GOD, your God, is with you every step you take" (Joshua 1:9, TM).

God commands us to not get discouraged, to avoid an attitude of timidity. God promises to fill us with abundant strength and courage, and He will hold our hands every step of the way. Just as God parted the Jordan River for Joshua and the Israelites to enter the Promised Land, He will guide and direct us throughout every obstacle. He unfolds our new journey one day at a time, one experience at a time.

Before setting out to slay giants, fight armed forces, build walls, or cross treacherous rivers, our biblical ancestors confirmed their goal with God. They prepared detailed plans. They analyzed the obstacles—giants, armed militia, floods, and famine. They accepted the missions set forth before them. We need to do the same thing. Here are practical steps to help you establish and maintain a clear focus.

Affirm your mission. Ensure that your goals and objectives are biblically sound by reading scripture. Pray big; verbalize your heart's desire to God.

Declare your goal. Say it out loud to yourself. Write your goal on a piece of paper, or record it in a file on your computer.

Create a plan. Detail necessary steps toward accomplishing your goal.

Maintain a hope-filled perspective. Don't get discouraged. Don't be timid. Record your minor and major successes.

Analyze obstacles. Study the specific environment encompassing your goal. Find out where the giants and other barriers dwell and how they might interfere with your plans.

Concentrate on the big picture. Don't get distracted. Make yourself accountable to someone you like and trust who will help you stay focused.

Goal-setting begins with a simple, easy-to-reach objective. Then progress to short-term and long-term goals. You'll discover that by following the steps above, your goal progresses from a blurred, out-of-reach mission to an attainable, crystal-clear vision. I encourage you to integrate effective goal-setting into your life so it becomes easy and natural. People who use goal-setting effectively suffer less stress and anxiety, focus on positive problem-solving, perform better, and feel motivated to overcome unforeseeable obstacles.

Unfortunately, fifty percent of the letters I mailed to adoption agencies came back marked "undeliverable" as more than twenty-five organizations had closed their doors. Several agencies responded with a letter indicating they no longer accepted applications because so few infants were available for adoption. A handful of responses stated that we were too old. One letter from a nun at a Catholic agency asked me to pray about the one and a half million abortions performed each year, as well as the socially acceptable trend of thirteen-year-old girls having babies and attempting to raise them.

Giants such as "too old" and astronomically high abortion rates caught us completely by surprise. After much prayer, we adjusted our plan, stayed focused, and surrounded ourselves with encouraging people.

Spend Time with Encouragers

How rare are those who sprinkle warm sunshine into the soul of a discouraged person through a gentle smile, a warm hand to hold, or a listening ear! Encouragers never judge the person or the situation. Encouragers have sensitive hearts and a ready word of support or inspiration, or a simple prayer that builds us up and equips us to face those giant-like obstacles. Let's face it—whether we're encountering adoption obstacles, health problems, job disruptions, parenting issues, or marital stress, we all need encouragement.

When you face obstacles, seek out encouragers. In fact, surround yourself with upbeat, positive people who will not only comfort you but also elevate your spirit. Our MADD friends cheered us on with supportive words and hugs. One friend bought me laugh-out-loud movies to watch. I'm not a craft-oriented person, but one precious senior lady from church encouraged me by teaching me how to cross-stitch. We started with bibs and progressed to adorable blankets. After much patient, love-filled instruction, I tackled sewing and embroidery on my own.

Do your best to avoid negative people when you're in dire need of encouragement, because negative people often offer negative advice. Input from pessimists may not be healthy for your *kardia*, and you may feel worse after talking with negative people. William Arthur Ward, author of *Fountains of Faith* and one of America's most quoted writers of inspirational maxims, wrote, "The pessimist borrows trouble; the optimist lends encouragement."

For the times when you're alone and need immediate encouragement, here are several tips to enhance your perspective:

- Read your Bible.
- Visualize your goal or vision. Cut out pictures from magazines that capture your goal or vision. Tape them next to your computer, or start a collection in a scrapbook.
- Read uplifting stories of heroes who overcame hindrances.
- Watch an inspiring movie.
- Go for a walk in a nature preserve or park.
- Pray for others.

Facing adoption obstacles wasn't easy by any means. But my friends and family filled me with the courage to keep knocking on doors. They provided unique ideas and fresh perspectives while comforting me. Isn't that what encouragement is really about?

Practice Patience

A small southern Missouri private adoption agency contacted us several months after our mailing. This agency sent a caseworker to our home to begin the evaluation process. The three of us sat at our antique oak kitchen table and sipped hot chocolate as the caseworker asked questions and took notes. She handed us a ream of paperwork and mentioned she had successfully placed several infants over the past few months. She expressed confidence that a birth mother would select us to parent her infant. Our names were placed on "potential adoptive parent" lists to be in front of judges and social workers for several sibling groups. We also made friends with pro-life pediatricians who promised to keep us in mind.

Bill and I completed the paperwork for the private agency within ten days and prayerfully mailed the packet to our new adoption caseworker. Several months later, our caseworker phoned us with the good news: a birth mother had chosen us to parent her baby.

"So what do we do now?" I asked.

"Get the nursery ready," she replied.

After hanging up the phone, Bill and I hugged while we wept tears of joy and thankfulness.

"Can you believe it, Honey?" I said. "We're going to be parents." We giggled and practiced calling each other Momma and Daddy while we bought furniture for our nursery. We ventured into baby stores, buying every cute item that touched our hearts. We decorated the nursery walls with red, blue, green, and yellow striped wallpaper. Bill surprised me with a blue velour swivel-type rocking chair. Friends and relatives purchased sleeping gowns, bibs, and receiving blankets for the precious little one we would soon call our own. Several weeks after the baby's due date, I finally phoned the caseworker for an update.

"I'm so sorry," she said. "I meant to phone you. The birth mother changed her mind. You know—family pressures. I'm working with several pregnant teens who plan to place their babies for adoption. Your baby is coming—it's just not born yet."

Two years later, still no baby or child. Bill said, "Honey, I can't stand watching your heartache. I think we need an emotional break. In the meantime, I'm shutting the door to our nursery."

I tried to say something, but my throat closed up. It hurt to swallow. My empty arms longed to hold "our baby." But my heart agreed with Bill; we desperately needed to step back and lighten the self-imposed emotional highs and lows. We grieved and continued to pray for God's favor. Through it all, He taught us many lessons, especially the virtue of patience.

But we continued to grow older with each passing year.

Perhaps you too have worn yourself out by trying to make things happen according to your own timing. Abel Bestavros, an Egyptian imprisoned because of his steadfast faith in Jesus, wrote about the many facets of patience, saying, "Patience with others is love. Patience with self is hope. Patience with God is faith."[3]

The Bible reminds us of the virtues of patience: "We know how troubles can develop passionate patience in us, and how that patience in turn forges the tempered steel of virtue, keeping us alert for whatever God will do next" (Romans 5:3, TM). Our planned and unplanned obstacles teach us that we are not in charge—God is. His Word promises that our patience lessons keep us alert for what God will do next.

Be Ready

For the next year my job duties broadened requiring longer hours and heavy travel. I didn't object, because my hectic schedule occupied my mind, consumed my time, and distracted my heart from the closed nursery door. My new constant prayer went something like this: *Lord, I'm prepared to be mom to an adoptive infant or child. I'm also prepared to accept whatever you deem best.* This prayer helped me brace myself for the best and the worst. It helped me maintain some sense of sanity while teaching me to surrender my will to our sovereign Creator.

* * *

*There are two kinds of people: those who say to God,
"Thy will be done," and those to whom God says,
"All right, then—have it your way."*

—C. S. Lewis

* * *

In the Lord's Prayer, Jesus taught His disciples to pray, "Your will be done on earth as it is in heaven" (Matthew 6:10). Submission to the Lord, praying that His will be done, minimizes our self-imposed anxiety that typically includes unrealistic deadlines and due dates. When we pray in accordance to God's will, we are relieved of our desire to single-handedly tackle obstacles.

Remember this: the difference in what we want and what God wants is often a matter of timing. We want obstacles removed right now. We want to achieve our goals today, tomorrow, or next week. Although God is working on these very things now, they may not fully happen until His perfect time.

Whatever obstacles you're facing, know that you do not face them alone. Jesus is right beside you, cheering you on, encouraging you to pray, *Your will be done*. Not only will you feel a sense of freedom, but you will also notice your perspective changing from fear-filled worry to positive anticipation.

Exhausted after a three-day business trip to Detroit, I argued with myself about whether to just call it a day and drive home or to go to the office. My work ethic won, so I drove to the office at 4:00 P.M. My phone rang as soon as I plopped my briefcase onto the floor. I motioned to my secretary to take a message. She got up from her desk and whispered, "It's MADD. They need you to speak tonight."

"Hi, Jan—this is Ina Fern. The Christian television station, Channel 50, called us, specifically requesting that you share your MADD testimony tonight. Can you make it?"

"Can't you get someone else to do it? I just returned from a grueling trip, and my brain is fried."

"Pray with me," she said.

We prayed. She had my full attention.

The next thing I knew I was sitting in the green room at the station. I picked up a brochure that read, "Pregnant? Distressed? There's hope!" I looked up and thought, *Are you talking to me?*

In my mind I heard, "Duh, Jan!"

Within an instant, my energy renewed. I shared my MADD testimony with the viewers, emphasizing how God comforts and rescues those who grieve. For the first time in public I said those gut-wrenching five words, "I'm no longer a mother." The phone lines lit up. Gracious callers thanked me for baring my soul. Several callers said my words inspired them and filled them with the courage to press on.

The next day while driving to work, I noticed the "Pregnant? Distressed?" brochure on the passenger seat. I put it into the pocket of my jacket for safekeeping.

Once in my office, I glanced at the phone messages stacked on my desk, each one requesting a return call. The brochure fell out as I took my jacket off. I picked it up and dialed the number.

"So this is a pro-life organization?" I asked.

"Yes. We're associated with Youth for Christ, and we offer guidance and counseling for unwed mothers," the voice on the other end said.

"Do any of the unwed mothers consider adoption?"

"Yes. We're also an adoption agency."

"Are you taking applications?"

"Yes."

"May I stop by and pick up an application?"

By noon I had arrived at the office, where I introduced myself to the agency director who graciously gave me a tour of the facilities and an adoption application packet.

I nearly skipped to my car and headed home to complete the paperwork.

Four weeks later, a precious lady from our new adoption agency phoned me.

"Are you sitting down?" she asked.

"Yes," I responded.

"Well, 'Mom,' your prayers have been answered."

I flipped backwards out of my office chair and smacked my head on the credenza, dropping the phone. I crawled on my hands and knees and picked up the receiver. Tears of joy streamed down my face. I placed my hand on my chest to calm my heart as I reminded myself to inhale and exhale.

"Really?" I asked.

"You're a mom, Jan! Your baby boy waits impatiently to meet you."

We named our baby boy Matthew, which means "gift from God." Oh, dear one, do not be discouraged when facing obstacles. God has great and glorious plans for our lives. He may not answer our prayer requests in accordance with our instant demands, but His timing is perfect.

The obstacles you face pale in comparison to God's all powerful love. Endure. Press on. Never give up. Keep your eye on the goal of God's will in your life.

Write your thoughts on what you've read.

_____

_____

_____

_____

_____

Questions

1. Read Norman Vincent Peale's words again, and describe how they can help you maintain a positive perspective in spite of your obstacles: "Stand up to your obstacles and do something about them. You will find that they haven't half the strength you think they have."

_____

_____

2. What discouragement and fear currently oppress your perspective?

_____

_____

3. How can seeking godly counsel help you?

_____

_____

4. What is praying small?

_____

_____

5. What is praying big?

_____

_____

6. What wisdom can you garner from George Mueller's prayer life?

_____

_____

7. Rephrasing, personalizing, and praying Bible verses encourage you to pray big. What can you experience when you pray in this manner?

_____

_____

8. I outlined six practical steps to help you establish and maintain a clear focus. Write a seventh one that personalizes this process for you.

_____

_____

9. When you need encouragement and you're alone, what actions can you take?

_____

_____

10. Abel Bestavros said, "Patience with others is love. Patience with self is hope. Patience with God is faith." How do these words encourage you?

_____

_____

11. What emotions did you feel at the end of this chapter?

_____

_____

7 ❋ LEARN TO GIVE AND RECEIVE LOVE

We have not come into the world to be numbered;
we have been created for a purpose; for great things:
to love and be loved.
—Mother Teresa

"Bill, hand me Matthew—I want to feel his heart next to mine," I said.

I lay face up, arms open wide, on our cozy, off-white couch. Bill gently placed our sleepy newborn on my chest. Our hearts pressed against one another, beating in near-perfect harmony. *Matthew, my precious son, God created you in my heart,* I whispered silently. Love tears filled my eyes and streamed down my face.

"How are you doing, Mom?" Bill asked.

I cried some more and then responded, "I can feel our baby's heartbeat. Dad, we're parents!"

Bill knelt on his knees next to our couch and placed one arm around me and one arm around Matthew. He squeezed my shoulder, closed his eyes, and prayed, "Oh, Lord Jesus, we thank you."

Our first afternoon home alone with Matthew, we giggled like little children, cried, and rejoiced. Earlier that day, a judge pronounced us legal parents of Matthew Jacob Coates. Finally, in the privacy of our home, parenthood seemed real. We held our baby, loved on him, and counted his toes and fingers. Matthew, our gift from God, ignited within us a sacred, agape love.

Have you ever held a newborn? If so, you can identify with the magical love that transpires through the touch of that silky smooth skin, the sound of soft coos, and the presence of innocence dependent upon nurturing love. How like God to make love so simple and accessible!

But somewhere along the path to adulthood, we make giving and receiving love complicated. Perhaps our hectic schedules, our insecurities, or our past experiences prevent us from getting on track with God's original design for us: to love and be loved. Whatever the reasons we've wandered away from love or neglected our need to give and receive love, it's time to move beyond the past to pursue our future. Apart from love, we cannot grow spiritually, emotionally, or personally. Love is a vital component in creating and maintaining a genuine, positive perspective.

I'm a work in progress; you're a work in progress. Jesus didn't come to make the perfect more perfect. He came to set us free so we can give and receive love. In this chapter we'll discover how to embrace God's perfect, unconditional love; how to fully love God; the importance of accepting ourselves; and how to put love into action.

To clear your head and prepare your heart for this exciting love adventure, please pray the prayer below.

Father, open the eyes of my heart so that I might know you and experience the depths of your love. Help me to remember that you know everything about me yet choose to love me. Teach me to know you intimately. Show me how to receive and share your everlasting love. Let me approach you with childlike faith and wonder. In your Son's name I pray. Amen

Embrace God's Love

Have you ever observed a toddler learning to walk? He or she waddles with arms extended horizontally in an effort to balance tiny steps. After a few strides toward Mommy, the little one tumbles into outstretched arms. The proud mommy claps and cheers, "Good job!"

Mommy's arms are always there just in time; she's always there to kiss away the hurts and respond to every need. That's exactly what God does. His perfect love pursues you with open arms prepared to catch you when you stumble, always ready to love you as you've never been loved before. He knows your every need. What does God desire from you? Our Heavenly Father yearns for you to embrace His love with childlike faith.

* * *

God is love. He didn't need us. But he wanted us.
And that is the most amazing thing.
—Rick Warren

* * *

The Bible is God's love letter to you, His child. Within its pages you'll discover God's messages of love, hope, and encouragement just for you! The excerpt below from "Father's Love Letter" paraphrases scripture to emphasize God's amazing love.

My Child

It is my desire to lavish my love on you.
1 John 3:1

My plan for your future has always been filled with hope.
Jeremiah 29:11

Because I love you with an everlasting love.
Jeremiah 31:3

I will never stop doing good to you.
Jeremiah 32:40

I am your Father, and I love you
even as I love my son, Jesus.
John 17:23

For in Jesus, my love for you is revealed.
John 17:26

His death was the ultimate expression
of my love for you.
1 John 4:10

I gave up everything I loved
that I might gain your love.
Romans 8:31-32

Love, Your Dad
Almighty God[1]

The entire "Father's Love Letter" is in the Appendix at the end of the book.

How do these words from "Father's Love Letter" make you feel? What does it tell you about God's love?

It's hard to describe, isn't it?

My journey to a new life began when I rededicated my life to Jesus on Easter Sunday in 1983. Grasping God's love is a process—it takes time to comprehend and embrace it. During the early stages of my journey I often measured God's love by my circumstances. We've all done it! If our jobs are secure, our relationships are intact, and everyday living is going well, we *wrongly* reason that it's because God is showering His love on us. Conversely, when we endure setbacks, painful health issues, or wounded relationships, we erroneously assume that God has forgotten us and doesn't love us. Here's the real truth: our circumstances constantly change. But God's love never changes. He remains close to us always. He always loves us, regardless of our circumstances, behaviors, and attitudes.

Note the following attributes and characteristics of God's almighty love.

- **God's love is eternal.** God himself is eternal, and God is love. His love for you will never cease. You can't do anything to hinder His love for you.

- **God's love is personal.** He desires a personal, loving relationship with you. You walk, talk, sleep, and work surrounded and saturated in His love. Every aspect of your life matters to God.

- **God's love is unconditional.** God's unconditional love does not require performance. It cannot be earned. It cannot be taken away.

- **God's love is perfect.** It is complete—nothing can be added or taken away from it. His love is the same yesterday, today, and throughout eternity.

- **God has no favorites.** God loves the sinner as much as He loves the saint. Individuals who accept God's invitation to a personal, loving relationship experience total intimacy with Him. This same divine intimacy is available to all just for the asking.

- **God's love is limitless.** Even those who are extra-needy won't exhaust God's love supply, because God's love knows no boundaries or limitations.

- **God's love is beyond human comprehension.** The human mind lacks the ability to understand God's love; it surpasses all knowledge. It can be difficult to comprehend, because God loves the sinner *but not the sin.* There's tremendous comfort in knowing you can't do anything to alter God's love for you.

Are you ready to embrace God's love with the wonder and awe of a child?

Loving God

Speaking for women's conferences and retreats allows me a wonderful opportunity to fellowship with women from all walks of life. It's a blessing to worship, minister, pray, and grow spiritually with fellow works-in-progress sisters. At a recent retreat in Coleman, Texas, the worship leader surprised us with childhood Sunday School sing-a-long songs. I glanced around the church sanctuary while we sang "Be Careful, Little Eyes" to see if the ladies were joining in and to observe their response. Big smiles adorned the precious faces of these special ladies. They pointed to their eyes as they sang, "Oh, be careful, little eyes, what you see." They pointed to their mouths, singing, "Be careful, little mouth, what you say." The women sang song after song, earnestly declaring their love of God with the straightforward faith of children. Several of the ladies were well past eighty, but they still remembered the words and hand motions of their treasured childhood songs.

Christian conferences, retreats, and our many churches create an environment conducive to praising, worshiping, and loving God. But how do we love God during the ninety-five percent of our time spent at home, work, parenting, running errands, cooking, and cleaning? How do we find God in the midst of our busyness? Observe the little child.

I began reading children's Bible books to Matthew when he was three weeks old. By the time he had graduated from the church nursery to preschool Sunday School, Matthew had memorized many of the stories and related Bible verses. By age three, he had begun talking to God. He chatted away, casually talking with God while playing with his wooden blocks, riding in his car seat, or playing outside in the backyard. His conversations went something like this: *Hi, God. I love you. Goodbye.*

One afternoon I found Matthew in his bedroom with a cardboard box and a marker. He asked me to write on a piece of paper "Baby Toys." He copied my letters with a few of them printed backwards onto the top flap of the box. He then asked me to leave the room. I left and pretended to walk down the hallway while silently listening and peeping through the doorway crack. Matthew gathered some of his older toys and a few books and tenderly placed them in the box. He then proceeded to talk with God: *God, will Baby like these?* Later he moved the box to a private spot under his bed.

Bill and I were still on a list to adopt a second baby from the same agency that placed Matthew with us. But after four years, we gave up hope because we had reached the age limit established by the agency. Matthew, however, didn't know what giving up hope meant. Every morning we ventured out to the gym where I participated in aerobics, and Matthew played in the childcare section with the other children. Matthew didn't like change. When he played at home, he wanted to stay there. Getting him out of the house always created a mild uproar. After settling him into his car seat, we held hands and prayed. Every single day, every single prayer, Matthew's requests revolved around "his" baby.

One morning four-year old Matthew strolled into my bedroom at 5:00 A.M., sporting his Batman pajamas with the cape flying behind him. He climbed into bed with me and said, "Guess who called me on the phone last night."

"Hmmm. Well, Matthew, was it Batman?"

"No, silly Mommy."

"I give up. Tell me who called you."

"God!"

"So, Son—what did God say to you?"

"He told me I have a baby!"

111

His words stirred a deep ache in my heart. *I should have told Matthew that we probably wouldn't be getting a baby,* I thought. *Now he's going to be so disappointed.* In an effort to steer the topic into another direction, I hugged Matthew and asked him if he wanted to visit the park after breakfast. My topic-change efforts had little impact.

Matthew told the daycare workers at the gym that God had made a baby for him. The workers later asked me if I was pregnant, to which I sadly replied that I was not. The following Sunday he told his Sunday School teacher the same story. Again, "Mrs. Coates, when is the baby due?" I forced a grin and said, "That Matthew has quite the imagination."

Two weeks after Matthew's divine declaration, I received a phone call from the adoption agency, informing me that we had been selected by a birth mom to parent her newborn. They couldn't provide specific details until certain legal issues had been resolved. But for sure, our second baby was indeed a reality.

As soon as I got off the phone with the agency, I said, "Matthew, guess what? We have a baby!"

"I already knew that, Mommy!"

The next day I so wanted to buy something pink or blue for our new baby but realized it made more sense to buy something neutral. On the way to the baby store I decided to really see if Matthew had a "hotline" to God.

"So, Matthew, did God tell you if we have a baby girl or a baby boy?"

"No!"

"Can you ask Him?"

"Okay."

Seated firmly in his car-seat, he snuggled against the door window with his back facing me. I stared at him, trying to figure out what he was doing.

"Don't look at me when I call God."

"Oh, okay."

Matthew scooted down in his seat, placing his hand against his ear as if holding a phone, and began to whisper.

Hi, God—it's me, Matt-u. No. Yes. Well, is my baby a boy or a girl? Okay. I love you, too. Bye, God.

Matthew straightened his posture and folded his hands on his lap.

"Well, what did God say?"

"He said He loves me! Oh, yeah—God told me He made me a baby girl."

As I grinned ear to ear, my heart danced with joy. Yes, we bought a pink dress at the baby store! Two weeks later, we flew from Boston to Kansas City to meet our new daughter. It was love at first sight for the Coates family. We named our precious, red-haired baby girl Jordan Nicole. Of course, Matthew insisted on being the first to hold his baby.

What can we, as adult women, learn about loving God from Matthew's childlike faith? I've listed below basic secrets to loving God with the abandon of a child.

- **Read scripture with enthusiastic passion.** Wrap your heart around truth, and hold it dear at all times. Insert your name in the stories to personalize verses. Delight in God's love through His Word. Believe it. Live it. "In your generous love I am really living at last!" (Psalm 63:3, TM).

- **Yearn for God's presence.** "As the deer pants for streams of water, so my soul pants for you, O God. My soul thirsts for

God, for the living God. When can I go and meet with God?" (Psalm 42:1-2).

- **Talk to God constantly.** God is available 24/7. Whisper prayers. Talk to God as your best friend and confidant. "Be cheerful no matter what; pray all the time; thank God no matter what happens" (1 Thessalonians 5:16-17, TM).
- **Trust in God.** Abandon your fears and inhibitions—God waits patiently for you to trust Him fully. "Whoever gives heed to instruction prospers, and blessed is he who trusts in the LORD" (Proverbs 16:20).
- **Obey God.** "This is love for God: to obey his commands. And his commands are not burdensome" (1 John 5:3).
- **Love God with all your heart.** Don't hold back. Give God all you have. "Love the Lord your God with all your heart and with all your soul and with all your mind" (Matthew 22:37).

I pray that God will speak to your heart directly about unique love lessons He wants you to glean from Matthew's love adventure.

Here's an awesome secret about the way God's love works: the more you get, the more you give! With all this supernatural loving going on, how on earth could anyone be down in the dumps and cloaked in a negative attitude?

Accept Yourself

Have you ever watched a group of young children sing a song for a school or church event? If so, you've probably noticed that many of the youngsters sing from their hearts as if they were the only one performing. Typically, they find their parents in the crowd, make eye contact, flash a gigantic smile, and sing away. Most of the kiddos are not old enough to worry about "image" issues; that blossoms somewhere between late grade-school age and puberty. And then watch out as the hormones kick in! Suddenly mirrors take on a whole new meaning. Just ask a preteen's relatives and friends. Do we ever outgrow this obsession with physical appearances?

Last fall I spoke to more than four hundred women at a weekend retreat in Michigan. During a small-group session I asked the ladies this question: "What one thing would you like to change about yourself?" Their responses included—

- My weight! I'd like to lose forty pounds.
- I wish I were fifteen years younger with no wrinkles.
- My kinky, wiry hair. I've always wanted soft, straight hair.
- My height. I hate being so tall.

One feisty lady responded to my question by asking me to answer my own question.

"Well," I stammered, "I don't know if you've noticed, but I'm under-tall. To be exact, I'm five feet, two inches and shrinking." The ladies laughed out loud and heartedly agreed with me.

"But, ladies, I'm working on it. I bought a grow-light in the nursery department at Wal-Mart. I sat under it for days, weeks—and nothing! I want my money back!" The ladies laughed some more, and several even clapped.

"You know what?" I continued. "God doesn't care about the outside. Sure, He wants us to take care of our bodies by eating the right foods and getting plenty of exercise and sleep. But when God looks at you, He sees you as His precious child. He doesn't mind that you're tall—or that I'm under-tall. He's truly interested in our hearts and the way we live our lives."

✳ ✳ ✳

What we are is God's gift to us.
What we become is our gift to God.
—Eleanor Powell

✳ ✳ ✳

God wants you to accept yourself for who you are: a wonderfully made, custom-designed child of God. Forget about those extra five pounds. Don't focus on the negative aspects of your physical appearance. Rather, focus on the gifts God gives you in order to live in a way that is pleasing to Him, to you, and to others.

The apostle Paul wrote, "But what happens when we live God's way? He brings gifts into our lives, much the same way that fruit appears in an orchard—things like affection for others, exuberance about life, serenity. We develop a willingness to stick with things, a sense of compassion in the heart, and a conviction that a basic holiness permeates things and people. We find ourselves involved in loyal commitments, not needing to force our way in life, able to marshal and direct our energies wisely" (Galatians 5:22-23, TM).

Accept your identity as a child of God. Graciously receive the gifts God brings into your life. Assume responsibility for who you are while asking God to help you grow the precious gifts of love, joy, peace, patience, kindness, goodness, faithfulness, gentleness, and self-control, which He so lovingly bestows upon you.

Put Love into Action

My daughter, Jordan, a tall, slender child, befriended Jane at our church's preschool program. Jane and Jordan held hands in line, played together on the outdoor swing set, and traded lunch items. Jordan's height enabled her to reach the light switch and the door knob for Jane. She delighted in retrieving toys and books from the shelf for Jane.

After two years of preschool, the five-year-old girls stood on the church's stage to receive their diplomas. The proud parents in the audience sat ready to applaud as their children accepted their diplomas. Jane gazed out at the audience, feeling the sting of stares, and froze. As she began to tremble, her tears turned to audible sobs.

Jordan stooped down and hugged her. Now, all eyes were on the two of them. The preschool director paused a few moments, walked over to Jordan and Jane, and whispered, "It's okay. Just remember—the people in the audience are your friends and family."

The preschool director reshuffled her alphabetized diplomas, placing Jordan's and Jane's together. She nodded at the two friends, and they walked across the stage hand in hand. Jordan hovered over Jane like a protective momma. The audience offered them a standing ovation as the girls accepted their diplomas.

Until the graduation ceremony, it never occurred to Jordan that Jane was different—they were first and foremost best friends. But Jane knew her dwarfism often stirred unwanted attention and stares. She experienced it as her family dined out or went to the movies. She sensed it that night on the stage. But the preschool director and Jordan and her fellow classmates rallied around Jane to demonstrate their love and support.

What would happen if we put away our biases and small thinking? What if we imitated Jordan's attitude of seeing others the way God sees them? Indeed, we would live in a "love is a verb" world! Here's what Ephesians 5:1-2 says about love in action:

Watch what God does, and then you do it, like children who learn proper behavior from their parents. Mostly what God does is love you. Keep company with him and learn a life of love. Observe how Christ loved us. His love was not cautious but extravagant. He didn't love in order to get something from us but to give everything of himself to us. Love like that (TM).

Basking in the love of God—soaking up His unlimited supply—enables us to share it with friends, family, and neighbors.

Several years ago a Fort Lauderdale, Florida, advertising agency launched a billboard campaign that included seventeen different messages from God. This nondenominational campaign, sponsored by an anonymous client, reminded us of what we already know but forget to do. Here's a message from this campaign I believe we need to heed:

"That 'Love thy neighbor' thing—I meant it."—God

"Love thy neighbor." It sounds so simple, doesn't it? For young children it is simple. Why? Little children stand in the love-receiving line. They freely accept love from their parents, family members, teachers, playmates, and most important, God. Their love for others flows from the love they receive.

Philip Carlson, author of *You Were Made for Love*, writes, "When our love does not flow from the well of love God has given, it will be obvious in our relationships. Our ability to be kind, generous, or otherwise loving to others will be lacking."[2]

On our own, we don't have the ability to love others, especially the difficult-to-love. But through the power of Jesus Christ, we can learn to love our neighbors. The more love we receive from our Creator, the more we put that love into action by loving our neighbors. Here are several simple tips to help you experience love in action:

- See others for who they are—God's creations.
- Practice humility.
- Be others-oriented.
- Do something nice for someone without expecting anything in return.
- Listen with your heart.
- Be generous with your hugs.
- Be patient with those around you—whether or not you know them.
- Treat others the way you want to be treated.
- Say, "I love you."

The more often you help someone else and let the love of Jesus shine within you, the better you'll feel. Loving others helps you build better relationships, enhances your intimacy capacity, removes your fears and inhibitions, helps you grow spiritually and emotionally, improves your quality of life, and stimulates lasting inner change. The more you love others, the more you help yourself experience a lifelong positive perspective.

Write your thoughts on what you've read.

_____

_____

_____

_____

Questions

1. In the first section of this chapter I wrote, "Apart from love, we cannot grow spiritually, emotionally, or personally." How do these words speak to your heart?

_____

_____

2. What paraphrased scripture did you enjoy most from "Father's Love Letter"? How does this verse help you embrace God's love?

_____

_____

3. What about Matthew's childlike faith did you most enjoy?

_____

_____

4. What is holding you back from loving God with all your heart?

_____

_____

5. "You are a wonderfully made, custom-designed child of God." How does this fact make you feel?

_____

_____

6. What can you do today to put love into action?

_____

_____

8 ✸ TAKE CHARGE OF YOUR THOUGHTS

The positive thinker sees the invisible, feels the intangible,
and achieves the impossible.
—Author unknown

"Ma'am, I'm not saying you can't build a home. I'm just saying it's a lot of work. You know—hammering nails, sawing wood. Sweat-equity home ownership isn't for everyone."

Esther adjusted her posture, prayed silently, and looked the manager of Self-Help Enterprises, Visalia, California, in the eyes.

"Yes, I understand hard work—may I have an application?" she asked.

A recently divorced mom of two, Esther yearned for a comfortable, affordable home for her family. Her limited budget couldn't stretch enough to cover Visalia's exorbitant home-apartment rental prices for more than a couple of months. She thoroughly researched dozens of home lease-to-purchase opportunities to no avail. Then a coworker of Esther's mentioned that he had recently received a new home loan through Self-Help Enterprises. He encouraged her to try it, saying, "You're a determined, hard-working woman. If I can do this sweat-equity thing, you can too."

Esther listened intently. "But, it's just me and my two young teenagers," she said.

He patted her on the back and said, "You can do it!"

His words echoed in her mind as she initiated internal pep talks: *I can do this. I can do this!*

Positive thinkers don't see obstacles; they see opportunities. When others see impossibilities, positive thinkers visualize possibilities. They rise above difficult situations while fixing their thoughts on "Whatever is true, whatever is noble, whatever is right, whatever is pure, whatever is lovely, whatever is admirable" (Philippians 4:8).

Don't beat yourself up if you haven't quite mastered the art of positive thought. Most of us aren't born with positive perspectives and smiles on our faces. That's a learned discipline that requires constant practice. In this chapter we'll equip you with the proper tools to help you change your thinking patterns. Notice I say "equip." You can read hundreds of positive self-help books and you can watch every motivational DVD on the planet. But you can still remain in a negative rut.

So what's the problem? Reading and listening are passive activities; you never actually *do* anything. Making positive thinking a reality requires your full commitment backed by intentional action. Let me repeat that: making positive thinking a reality requires your full commitment backed by intentional action. Like Esther's new home opportunity, taking charge of your thoughts while developing self-discipline happens when you incorporate a "sweat equity" mentality.

Think "Sweat Equity"

Esther sat at her kitchen table and analyzed the loan application and many other forms. She bought file folders, spiral notebooks, and pens at a nearby office supply store. She pulled out the first file folder, neatly printing "Our New Home" on the tab. She grabbed a pen and spiral notebook to outline the Self-Help Enterprises program requirements. Here's a sample of her notes:

- Houses are available to families who *qualify* for loans. Low-interest loans are available.
- I don't have to have construction knowledge.

- A site construction superintendent trains the families in work that includes preparing the foundation, concrete finishing, framing, electrical, painting, and landscaping.
- Families provide sixty-five percent of the labor.
- Each family is required to put in forty hours a week for the duration of the project, which can take up to ten months.
- Subcontractors handle the more complex parts of the construction, including cabinets, HVAC, roofing, plumbing, stucco, and flooring.
- Ten families work together to finish the ten homes. No one moves in until all the homes are completed.

Esther paused a few moments, then flipped her spiral notebook to a blank page, titling it "Current Weekly Time Commitments." Her entries included forty hours at her job, two hours at church. Sighing deeply, she placed her hands over her aching, knotted stomach. Shadows of doubt and fear lingered in her mind. She stood up from her chair, paced around the table, sat back down, grabbed her pen, and added this notation to her current weekly time commitments: "forty hours—build our new home."

What does sweat-equity home ownership have to do with taking charge of your thoughts? Both require an investment of time, concentrated labor, and a desire to move forward by creating a new reality. Are you tired of being mired in the same negative thought patterns that have plagued you your whole life? Are you frustrated with your lack of progress? Have you had enough of the status quo? Are you irritated enough to make some changes? Are you ready to take charge of your thought life? Are you willing to get rid of your bad thought habits in order to experience positive, healthy thinking? If so, my friend, pray the prayer below.

God, fill me with a desire to take charge of my thoughts. I yearn to fix my thoughts on what is true and honorable. I want my thought life to glorify you. Help me get out of my comfort zone and become a positive thinker.

Esther worked hard to complete the lengthy loan application forms and finally received approval to move forward with the building project. Congratulating her, the Self-Help superintendent shook her hand and said, "Here's the blueprint for your new home." She thanked him and headed for the door, tears of thankfulness streaming down her face. "Wait," he called after her, pointing to her new equipment—tool belt, ladder, tools, and instruction pamphlets. "We're starting work soon. You'll need these. In the meantime, review the blueprints."

Study the Blueprints

Can you imagine building a home without professional blueprints? Structures would be off-balance and unsafe. Blueprints are the difference between a satisfactory product and a disastrous project. Blueprints contain specific construction details and important information about the project size. Without them, we can't build solid, well-built, permanent structures. They provide a reliable reference source for all involved in the construction process, insuring owner confidence and satisfaction as well as a successful project.

But how many times do we venture off into our day without any thought to our custom-designed blueprints? God designed us to "Be cheerful no matter what; pray all the time; thank God no matter what happens. This is the way God wants you who belong to Christ Jesus to live" (1 Thessalonians 5:16-18, TM). But our thoughts often get in the way of living out God's plans for our lives.

Researchers estimate that the average human has approximately 12,000 to 50,000 thoughts per day. What you think about powerfully impacts who you are. I recently asked workshop participants to turn to the persons next to them and ask, "How are you?" Here are some of the answers people gave:

"Okay."

"Not too bad."

"Oh, I guess so-so."

"Great!"

"Don't even ask!"

"All things considered, I'll get by."

Summed up, the responses represent neutral, negative, and positive. How do you answer when someone asks how you are doing? Regardless of our past experiences, our current situation, or our worries about the future, our Creator's blueprints remind us that we are blessed. If you don't believe me, read Matthew 5:3-10 (TM):

- You're blessed when you're at the end of your rope.

  With less of you there is more of God and his rule (verse 3).

- You're blessed when you feel you've lost what is most dear to you.

  Only then can you be embraced by the One most dear to you (verse 4).

- You're blessed when you're content with just who you are—no more, no less.

  That's the moment you find yourself proud owner of everything that can't be bought (verse 5).

- You're blessed when you've worked up a good appetite for God.

  He's food and drink in the best meal you'll ever eat (verse 6).

- You're blessed when you care.

  At the moment of being "care-full," you find yourself cared *for* (verse 7).

- You're blessed when you get your inside world—your mind and heart—put right.

  Then you can see God in the outside world (verse 8).

- You're blessed when you can show people how to cooperate instead of compete or fight.

  That's when you discover who you really are and see your place in God's family (verse 9).

- You're blessed when your commitment to God provokes persecution.

  The persecution drives you even deeper into God's kingdom (verse 10).

Read these blessings found in the Book of Matthew again and again. Memorize them. Remind yourself repeatedly that you are blessed in every negative, neutral, and positive life situation. Our Master Architect designs every area of our lives with abundant love, mercy, grace, and blessings. Sometimes we become so distracted by our problems that negativity consumes us.

In her devotional book *Jesus Calling,* Sarah Young writes as if Jesus were speaking directly to the reader. Here's what she notes about blessings: "I shower blessings on you daily, but sometimes you don't perceive them. When your mind is stuck on a negative focus, you see neither Me nor My gifts. In faith, thank Me for whatever is preoccupying your mind. This will clear the blockage so that you can find Me."[1]

I pray your response in the future when you're asked how you're doing will be "I'm blessed!" Read the fine print of God's blueprints for life—then follow the directions. Apply these carefully written, life-renewing scriptures to every area of your life, make note of how much God loves you, and progress toward a new you with a positive perspective.

Record Progress

The construction superintendent called a special meeting for the ten families—including Esther's—to review the workflow process, discuss safety issues, review the proper use and care of tools, and share tips on recruiting volunteers. The seasoned supervisor thoroughly covered every detail.

He then asked the ten families to introduce themselves to each another. The introduction made Esther feel understaffed and insignificant, because she was the only female head of the household in the work group. She also had the smallest family. Each of the nine married couples had three or more children to help them accumulate the necessary forty hours per week and provide moral support. The superintendent handed each family a black work-log booklet. "You must record your weekly hours," he said.

Esther's hands shook as she flipped through the one-hundred-plus lined pages in her work log booklet and thought, *What have I done?* Esther glanced at her two teenagers. Ernie firmly held the shiny new hammer, and Jonna Lea extended the metal measuring tape as if to show Esther she could do it. Driving home, Esther explained to her kids the importance of recording their hours. She later gave them each a pocket-sized notebook and explained that at the end of each week she would transfer their hours to the work log.

Ernie recruited his friends to help. Jonna's school band members pitched in. Esther's coworkers supported her efforts by volunteering to work with her throughout the project. With the help of family, friends, and coworkers, the entries in Esther's work log grew. And so did her confidence that she would realize her dream of home ownership.

Intentionally tracking progress is a positive discipline for all of us. In order to monitor our 5,000-50,000 daily thoughts, we must practice logging them. I asked Esther for a sampling of her thought log during those weeks she worked forty hours for her employer and forty hours on her future home. Here's what she provided:

Situation	Thoughts
Blaring construction noise vibrates my head.	• This is going to destroy my eardrums. • I feel a migraine coming on. • Oh, for some peace and quiet!
Brought cassette player with praise-and-worship music tape to construction site.	• Thank you, Lord!
Ran out of drinking water.	• I'll never make it through the next hour.
Fellow building team member brought a six-gallon water jug. He saw my distress and handed me a cool, refreshing cup of water. He told me to drink all the water I need.	• I'm humbled by my team member's generosity and kindness.
Night shift at employer.	• Sane people are in bed sleeping.
Physically exhausted.	• 1,000 more hours to go. • I don't know how I'll make it.
Took an afternoon off.	• I so needed a brief break.
Messed up on wiring.	• I've never done this before. • The superintendent needs to be more patient with me.
Team member fixed my wiring problem.	• I'm thankful I work with helpful people.
Maria brought me homemade tortillas.	• My work team is becoming like family.
Inspector called for "hurricane clips" to be hammered to strengthen framework. I was almost finished with the last house. While applying the clips, I missed the target and slammed my forefinger with the hammer. The severe pain caused me to vomit. Doc fitted me with a brace. After I regained my composure, I went back to work.	• I'm never building another house. • Where's my work team? • God, give me strength. • I'm too far into this to quit— besides that, I don't have any choice. • I can do this. • This, too, shall pass.

This is an abbreviated version of the log of Esther's thoughts. But you get the picture: she experienced a full range of thoughts—positive, negative, neutral—throughout the ten months it took to build her home. It's interesting to note that she brought her thoughts full circle to help her focus on the positive perspective of building her home.

Logging our thoughts allows us to honestly review our positive, neutral, and negative thought processes. It reveals thought patterns that can be damaging and sometimes dangerous. It allows us to observe our thoughts and become aware of what's going on in our minds; we can't manage and minimize negative thoughts if we're not aware of them. Recording our thoughts helps us separate *feelings* (which are rarely accurate) from *fact*. It also helps us acknowledge negative thoughts and situations so we can consciously choose neutral or—even better—positive thoughts.

Copy the format below onto a piece of paper, or write on this page. Record your thoughts for fifteen to twenty minutes. Notice I've added a column so you can label the thought as negative, neutral, or positive.

Situation	Thoughts	Negative, Neutral, or Positive

This exercise is meant to introduce you to the thought-logging process. With your sincere cooperation and input, you are well on your way to taking charge of your thoughts. Hint: recording your progress also provides encouragement.

Following are some tips to help minimize your negative thought patterns while boosting the positives on your thought log:

- Eliminate expressions like *never, should, can't,* and *if only* from your vocabulary.
- Focus on what you want to do rather than what you don't want to do.
- When you're complimented, say, "Thank you."
- Tame your tongue by quitting negative, destructive self-talk.
- Treat your internal musings as if they are an uplifting conversation with a good friend.
- Stop whining and complaining.
- Practice self-control.
- Don't take everything personally.
- Count your blessings.
- Eliminate intentional negative input—like televised news—before bedtime.
- Smile more.
- Say no to negativity.
- Think through your problems—diagnose them. Respond rather than react.
- Choose to be positive.

- Play upbeat music.
- Remember: while you can't control what happens to you, you can control, with God's help, how you respond to what happens to you.
- When someone says something to you that could be taken as a positive or a negative, give him or her the benefit of the doubt, and assume the person meant it in a positive light.

Experts say it takes twenty-one days to break a bad habit or replace a negative pattern with a positive one, so be patient with yourself. Apply sweat-equity to your thinking process by working hard to think about wholesome, healthy things. Focus on your progress. Remember: God loves you just as you are, but He loves you too much to leave you that way.

Use the Right Tools

The superintendent gave Esther the correct tools to complete the job. She didn't hide them under her bed in hopes that her home would get built. She faithfully used her saw, hammer, level, pliers, wrench, shovel, measuring tape, drill, and more every day. Far too often we leave our God-tools on the nightstand next to our bed, leaping toward each day totally unprepared to keep our thoughts focused on what is godly, pure, and healthy. The apostle Paul reminds us that we need to refocus our minds from the horizontal to the vertical. "We use our powerful God-tools for smashing warped philosophies, tearing down barriers erected against the truth of God, fitting every loose thought and emotion and impulse in to the structure of life shaped by Christ" (2 Corinthians 10:4-5, TM). We need to move beyond human everyday worries and get on with thoughts that really matter: pursuing a life shaped by Christ.

Some people immediately understand and connect with this life-shaped-by-Christ idea. I guess I'm a slow learner. I read and reread the Bible in an effort to put God's tools to work in my life. When I finally began to grasp my new identity in Christ—a daughter of the King, accepted, secure, significant—I began to experience the fullness and blessings of a life in Christ. My thought life transformed from partly positive to mostly positive as I applied God's truth to my life. Read the Word of God that follows—your God tools—to affirm who you are.

Who I Am in Christ[2]

I am accepted . . .

John 1:12	I am God's child.
John 15:15	As a disciple, I am a friend of Jesus Christ.
Romans 5:1	I have been justified.
1 Corinthians 6:17	I am united with the Lord, and I am one with Him in spirit.
1 Corinthians 6:19-20	I have been bought with a price, and I belong to God.
1 Corinthians 12:27	I am a member of Christ's body.
Ephesians 1:3-8	I have been chosen by God and adopted as His child.
Colossians 1:13-14	I have been redeemed and forgiven of all my sins.
Colossians 2:9-10	I am complete in Christ.
Hebrews 4:14-16	I have direct access to the throne of grace through Jesus Christ.

I am secure . . .

Romans 8:1-2	I am free from condemnation.
Romans 8:28	I am assured that God works for my good in all circumstances.
Romans 8:31-39	I am free from any condemnation brought against me, and I cannot be separated from the love of God.
2 Corinthians 1:21-22	I have been established, anointed, and sealed by God.
Colossians 3:1-4	I am hidden with Christ in God.
Philippians 1:6	I am confident that God will complete the good work He started in me.
Philippians 3:20	I am a citizen of heaven.

2 Timothy 1:7	I have not been given a spirit of fear but of power, love, and a sound mind.
1 John 5:18	I am born of God, and the evil one cannot touch me.
	I am significant . . .
John 15:5	I am a branch of Jesus Christ, the true vine, and a channel of His life.
John 15:16	I have been chosen and appointed to bear fruit.
1 Corinthians 3:16	I am God's temple.
2 Corinthians 5:17-21	I am a minister of reconciliation for God.
Ephesians 2:6	I am seated with Jesus Christ in the heavenly realm.
Ephesians 2:10	I am God's workmanship.
Ephesians 3:12	I may approach God with freedom and confidence.
Philippians 4:13	I can do all things through Christ, who strengthens me.

Great tools for your thought life! Remember: the more you reaffirm who you are in Christ, the more your thought life will begin to reflect your true identity.

Lay a Strong Foundation

"The backhoe tractor broke down," the superintendent said. "It should be repaired within a couple of days. The bad news is that the concrete is scheduled to be poured by the end of the week, so grab your shovels and start digging."

The 110-degree temperature and blistering sun scorched Esther's arms and shoulders. She walked across the street to rest a moment in the shade of a mature oak tree. She glanced toward the sky as she sat cross-legged on the ground. The sting of salty perspiration from her brow trickled into her eyes. *Jesus, I need strength—you are my firm foundation,* she prayed. Her work team members sensed her weariness. They grabbed shovels and began leveling the hot soil on

Esther's lot. She blinked her burning eyes several times, noticing her team's laborious efforts. *They are so kind. Thank you, Lord.*

Every structure, whether it's a home, church, office, or school, requires a solid, well-engineered foundation. The quality of the ground preparation determines the stability of the structure. Similarly, taking charge of our thoughts means laying a strong foundation within our *kardia* (heart, mind, body and soul) with unshakable faith in the Creator, who spoke this world into being. "The fundamental fact of existence is that this trust in God, this faith, is the *firm foundation* under everything that makes life worth living. It's our handle on what we can't see. The act of faith is what distinguished our ancestors, set them above the crowd" (Hebrews 11:1, TM, emphasis added).

Esther couldn't see or touch her home, yet she could envision it. She couldn't physically see Jesus, yet she prayed to Him. She placed her trust not in the shovels and concrete but in Jesus. A. W. Tozer wrote, "If our faith is to have a firm foundation, we must be convinced beyond any possible doubt that God is altogether worthy of our trust."[3]

While placing your faith and trust in God, envision a new you. Believe in it. Pray about it. Work at it. A solid foundation will keep you from caving in when storms hit. It will get you through the ups and downs of life while maintaining a wholesome thought life.

Think About It

Esther listened to praise-and-worship tapes to fill her *kardia* with positive truth while building her home. She overcame the many home construction challenges by filling her mind with the Word of God and offering continual prayer. When faced with discouragement and fatigue, she acknowledged her feelings and reframed her thoughts. In other words, she replaced negative thinking with positive thinking. She kept her eye on the goal: an affordable, comfortable home for her family. She kept mental images of her home, complete with trees and flowers, in the forefront of her mind.

Researchers agree that outer-world images, sound, light, darkness, odors, and colors stir individual internal responses. Psychologists call these reactions *triggers*. Dwelling on negative situations that trigger negative emotions defeats our goals and objectives. It breeds negative thoughts. Conversely, thinking about pure and lovely images, colors, and sounds stimulates positive responses. Ponder these images:

- A graceful Monarch butterfly flitting about a golden daisy with background grasses dancing in perfect rhythm to spring's gentle breeze.
- The first smile of a new baby.
- A late-afternoon sky decorated with a pastel rainbow.
- A crystal-clear waterfall framed with electric green trees and vibrant, multicolored wildflowers.
- A soft, white dove perched on a limb, chirping a love song.

I hope these images stir thoughts of beauty, peacefulness, and God's precious creations in your mind.

Several years ago I planted a violet Texas Vitex tree in the garden beneath my office window. Its fragrant blossoms invite a parade of bees and butterflies throughout the summer and autumn. Hummingbirds flutter about its blossoms as they sip the sweet nectar. God transformed this common tree into a beautiful backdrop to display His creatures. Loveliness is everywhere if we take time to notice it and view it from God's perspective. Here are tips to help you take charge of your thoughts and transform negative thinking to positive thinking.

- **Focus on the right things.** "Fix your thoughts on what is true and honorable" (Philippians 4:8).

- **Allow God to constantly renew your mind.** "Do not conform any longer to the pattern of this world, but be transformed by the renewing of your mind. Then you will be able to test and approve what God's will is—his good, pleasing and perfect will" (Romans 12:2).

- **Disable wrong thoughts.** "We demolish arguments and every pretension that sets itself up against the knowledge of God, and we take captive every thought to make it obedient to Christ" (2 Corinthians 10:5).

- **Accept peace.** "I am leaving you with a gift—peace of mind and heart. And the peace I give is a gift the world cannot give. So don't be troubled or afraid" (John 14:27, NLT).

I hope these resources will help you overcome any present and future thinking challenges. Stick some Post-its throughout this scripture-filled chapter to use for future reference. Highlight and memorize these verses to keep them close to your heart. Taking charge of your thoughts is a moment-by-moment process with delightful rewards. Envision your new life with healthy thought patterns. Believe it. Work at it. Think about it. Actualize it.

Esther and her two kids moved into their home ten months after project initiation. Twenty years later, Esther still lives in her home, which was paid in full by sweat equity and timely payments on her mortgage loan. Her positive perspective continues to radiate in all she does and thinks. How do I know all these intimate details of this special lady's life? She's my baby sister. I'm so proud of her, and I pray that you're blessed by her story.

Write your thoughts on what you've read.

_____

_____

_____

Questions

1. "Positive thinkers don't see obstacles; they envision opportunities. When others see impossibilities, positive thinkers visualize possibilities." How can these powerful words impact the way you view situations?

_____

_____

2. What does "sweat-equity" have to do with taking charge of your thoughts?

_____

_____

3. Read Matthew 5:3-10, located in the "Study the Blueprints" section again. Then write your response to "How are you doing?" below.

_____

_____

4. Thought-logging allows you to examine your thoughts and become aware of what is going on in your mind. Identify three additional benefits of thought-logging.

_____

_____

5. "God loves you just as you are, but He loves you too much to leave you that way." How do these words make you feel?

_____

_____

6. List your three favorite verses from "Who I Am in Christ."

_____

_____

7. "The fundamental fact of existence is that this trust in God, this faith, is the firm foundation under everything that makes life worth living. It's our handle on what we can't see. The act of faith is what distinguished our ancestors, set them above the crowd" (Hebrews 11:1, TM). In what ways does this verse speak to you?

_____

_____

8. In what ways did Esther's homebuilding story encourage you?

_____

_____

9 ✸ TRANSFORM FROM THE INSIDE OUT

What the caterpillar calls the end of the world,
the master calls a butterfly.

—Richard Bach

Blizzard-like weather conditions nearly blinded me as I exited the dark, underground parking garage in downtown Kansas City. I pulled up to the cashier and rolled down my window to pay my parking fee.

My boss, Mike, joked, "Ten bucks if you hit the bag lady."

I ignored him and focused on the cashier transaction. I pulled forward and then slammed on the brakes to avoid hitting the woman four feet in front of my car. She wore two woolen hats, mismatched mittens, a raggedy coat, and white tennis shoes with holes. When I glanced into her piercing blue eyes, I recognized her. Bertha. Random thoughts raced through my mind. *Oh, Lord, I almost hit her. Why did she walk away as if nothing happened? Why didn't she beat her fists on the hood of my car or shout cuss words?*

Years ago Bertha had been a pampered suburban housewife with a maid. Then paranoid schizophrenia and manic depression took her in and out of mental institutions and ultimately to a life as a bag lady. Shock treatments, drug use, and alcohol abuse had made her life a living hell. Well-meaning pastors, doctors, nurses, family, and friends labeled her hopeless.

After many years of out-of-control turbulence, Bertha's family reached a difficult but wise decision. By making her a ward of the state, she lived in a safe, secure, government-subsidized apartment in the downtown area of Kansas City. She liked her apartment but found it difficult to stay there for any length of time. I often saw her plodding through the streets with a black plastic trash bag firmly gripped in each hand. She mined dumpsters, seeking treasures to fill her trash bags and apartment. She lashed out verbally at anyone within listening distance. She would tangle with an angry bull if he got in her way.

After the incident in front of the parking garage, I dropped Mike off at the office. As I drove a few blocks and parked my car, I prayed for the Lord's guidance. *I don't know how to help her, so I'm asking you to do it.*

In an effort to regain my composure, I rested my head on the steering wheel for a few moments. I made a decision to buy a few things for Bertha. I drove to a farm supply store near the Kansas City Stockyards, just west of the downtown area, and purchased insulated boots and ski gloves for Bertha. A small corner grocery store was still open, so I went in and bought bread, cold cuts, milk, and crackers. I loaded the clothes and food into my car. My windshield wipers couldn't keep up with the heavy snowfall. I navigated the ice-packed streets and located the apartment building I knew she had lived in at one time.

I was relieved to see her name still on the mailbox. I knocked on the brown metal door, and Bertha opened it, wearing a well-worn man's blue plaid shirt and polyester pants with unsightly snags. She flashed a huge, toothless grin and welcomed me with a warm hug. Her out-of-character cheerfulness and hug startled me.

"I brought you some goodies," I explained, "so take out the beer to make room in the refrigerator, okay?"

"Oh, no beer. No drugs either!"

I raised my eyebrows in surprise. "Really?"

"Yes! I have friends now and a job. In fact, I'm having dinner with my friends tonight. Wanna come?"

This I had to see! "Sure," I responded.

Sure enough, there was no beer to be seen in her refrigerator as I put away the few things I had bought. Pleasantly surprised, I looked at her again. She seemed different, but I couldn't pinpoint what it was. *Perhaps she's found a "happy" drug*, I thought.

"We need to hurry," she said. "Dinner is always at six-thirty."

Bertha slipped on the new boots I had bought her and danced around the small living room. We bundled up and headed for my car.

"Tell me how to get wherever it is we're going," I said.

"Go straight. Turn left. No, turn right. Keep going. We're here!"

The sign on the building read "The Salvation Army."

I parked the car and walked around to the passenger door to open it for Bertha. Smiling, she looped one arm into mine and grabbed a half-full black plastic trash bag with her free hand. We trudged through the deep snow and into The Salvation Army building, where officers in uniform loved on Bertha with hugs and sincere smiles. They seated us at a wooden table and volunteered to get our food.

Bertha hummed and winked at me. *What is going on here?* I wondered. I picked at my food while Bertha dove into hers as if she hadn't eaten in three days. She put her left arm around me and squeezed. With her right arm she reached across my plate, snatched my dinner roll, and dropped it into her trash bag. She then tilted my chin to face her. She looked me in the eye, her own eyes twinkling.

"I love you, Jan!"

My throat tightened.

For the first time in my entire life, my mother and I connected at the heart level.

You've heard the adage, "Sometimes it takes an army." Well, in Mom's case, it took a very special army to do what shock treatments, tranquilizers, and dozens of doctors couldn't do. Through the love of Jesus, the saints of The Salvation Army loved on Mom, craziness and all. They fed her nutritional food for her body as well as spiritual food for her soul.

Mom had rededicated her life to Jesus and began to experience transformation from the inside out. Soon she radiated a peace that passes all understanding. She received love from others with open arms and a receptive heart, and she learned how to extend love to others. The Salvation Army helped Mom get sober and reconcile with her family. Mom's newfound commitment to Christ earned her the right to become an official soldier in the Army. She humbly wore her navy blue uniform, and her new life revolved around Army activities, including Bible study, summer camp, bell-ringing, and special activities.

Mom's transformation would not have been possible without divine intervention. But she, too, had to make—and keep—life-changing commitments in order to transform her adversities to positivity, including—

- Surrendering control of her life to God
- Accepting a new heart and a new spirit
- Embracing hope

God still performs transformations. He alone can transform a caterpillar to a butterfly, and He alone can help you transform your adversities into positivity.

How can you become a butterfly? First, you must truly want to fly. Second, you must be willing to give up being a caterpillar. Giving up caterpillar status means that you surrender your trials and sorrows to God, who will in His perfect time make them as good as new (Zechariah 10:6).

Surrender Control

The graceful butterfly lays eggs that hatch into slimy, green caterpillars. The caterpillar doesn't comprehend its future metamorphosis as it squirms aimlessly along leafy branches and green plants. It eats and eats, growing to many times its original size. It then spins a cocoon and goes through growth stages, ending in one called "chrysalis."

As chrysalis, the caterpillar dissolves into a liquid blob incapable of doing anything. The term is derived from the metallic gold coloration found in the "pupa" of many butterflies. In his book *Sit Stand Walk,* Watchmen Nee wrote, "God is waiting till you cease to do. God is waiting for your store of strength to be utterly exhausted before he can deliver you. Once you have ceased to struggle, he will do everything."[1]

When we become "pupa"—liquid gold in God's hands—unable to struggle, we can expect new life transformation.

Mom originally visited The Salvation Army because she had heard about the free food. Not only did she eat the food, but she also brought her ever-present black plastic trash bags with her in hopes of stuffing them with as much as she could get away with. One kind officer informed Mom that she could bring only one trash bag into the dining area. She reluctantly surrendered her second bag near the entrance. Another officer took Mom aside and kindly asked her to refrain from stealing food from the food line. The officer encouraged Mom to take what she could eat, and if others had leftover dinner rolls, she could ask them for permission to take their rolls home with her. Mom willingly abandoned her unacceptable social skills and accepted the Army's code of conduct so she could remain in good standing with her new friends who accepted and loved her.

Next, Mom enrolled in Bible study. She memorized scripture, actively participated in the discussion questions, and with the help of patient, loving teachers, discovered how to apply God's precepts to her life. As she became more and more familiar with the Word of God, she finally understood that God didn't see her as "hopeless." He saw her as a hope-filled child of God.

* * *

Hope is faith holding out its hand in the dark.
—George Illes

* * *

Within several months, my mother rededicated her life to Jesus. By doing this, she intentionally relinquished control of her life and became "liquid gold" in God's hands. God kept her in His safe embrace as she released the strongholds of alcohol and drugs. She emerged from God's cocoon as a grace-filled butterfly who planted seeds of love, joy, and peace in the lives of others.

For most of us, surrender can create fear and confusion, because we often associate surrender with losing a battle or giving in. Think of surrender to God more as an action of *giving over* control, in love, to Him. The apostle Paul wrote, "Throw yourselves wholeheartedly and full-time . . . into God's way of doing things" (Romans 6:13, TM).

Perhaps you're struggling with releasing control of your life to God. Here are several steps of surrender.

- **Give God free reign in your life.** Hand Him full control. Releasing control of your life to God is a lifelong process. Remind yourself moment by moment that you live a life surrendered to God. Allow Him to guide you continually. "The LORD will guide you always" (Isaiah 58:11).
- **Depend on God.** Live a life contingent on God. "Listen for God's voice in everything you do, everywhere you go; he's the one who will keep you on track" (Proverbs 3:6, TM).

- **Abandon a self-centered life for the God-centered life.** Stop focusing on yourself, and seek what God has for you. Our perfect example of a surrendered, God-centered life is seen in Jesus Christ himself. "Every person the Father gives me eventually comes running to me. And once that person is with me, I hold on and don't let go. I came down from heaven not to follow my own whim but to accomplish the will of the One who sent me" (John 6:37-38, TM).

- **Live a "want to" life, not a "have to" life.** Serve God because you desire to serve Him. Want to live a life of freedom? Want to embrace more of God and less of you? Want to experience a new life? Then drop the chains of bondage by surrendering the old you for a new you. "So don't you see that we don't owe this old do-it-yourself life one red cent? There's nothing in it for us, nothing at all. The best thing to do is give it a decent burial and get on with your new life. God's Spirit beckons. There are things to do and places to go" (Romans 8:12-14, TM).

Think about it. Surely no one wants to live like a caterpillar. I know I don't. I want to be liquid gold in God's hands so I can be free to spread glorious wings like a butterfly and enjoy the great God-filled adventure before me. Join me—you'll love the ride!

Receive a New Heart

The evening I had dinner with Mom and the saints of The Salvation Army was only four short months after my son, Chris, was killed by a drunk driver. I was still in the throes of raw grief. But witnessing Mom's transformation trumped my inner numbness.

How could her heart have been so drastically changed? How did her inability to love God and others change to childlike love for God and those she came in contact with? How was her negative, bitter attitude transformed into an attitude of gratitude filled with positivity? Six simple words provide the amazing answer: *God gave her a new heart.*

God's Word says it so beautifully: "I'll give you a new heart, put a new spirit in you. I'll remove the stone heart from your body and replace it with a heart that's God-willed, not self-willed. I'll put my Spirit in you and make it possible for you to do what I tell you and live by my commands" (Ezekiel 36:26-27, TM).

✳ ✳ ✳

The most beautiful things in the world are not seen or touched. They are felt with the heart.

—Helen Keller

✳ ✳ ✳

Looking back in the rearview mirror of my life, I realize that Mom's metamorphosis was a major turning point for me. Easter Sunday 1983, two months after I had dinner with Mom at The Salvation Army, Bill and I publicly accepted Jesus as Lord and Savior of our lives. My own metamorphosis began.

God replaced my beyond-repair, corrupt, stony heart with a new *kardia* (heart, mind, body, and spirit). My new *kardia* depends on the Holy Spirit, who resides in me to pump new life into me every time I inhale. Like the butterfly, I'm able to flutter my wings about, planting seeds in God's kingdom throughout the day.

I don't fully know or understand what trips you up. But God does, and He has the perfect solution: a new heart with a lifetime guarantee that allows moment-to-moment do-overs! When you accept the precious gift of a new heart and a new spirit, God promises to help you move forward in your new life transformation. Here are steps to help you fully experience this new heart process.

- **Accept His gift of a new heart.** Thank the Lord for loving you so much that He discards all the junk in your old heart by replacing it with a new one. Be a cooperative patient as the Great Physician performs your heart transplant. "I will give you a new heart and put a new spirit in you" (Ezekiel 36:26).

- **Rest in the Lord.** Become liquid gold in God's hands while He breathes new life into your *kardia* (heart, soul, mind, and spirit). "This means that anyone who belongs to Christ has become a new person. The old life is gone; a new life has begun!" (2 Corinthians 5:17).

- **Trust God with all your heart.** Your Creator knows what is best for you and has the power to make the best happen in your life. "Trust God from the bottom of your heart; don't try to figure out everything on your own" (Proverbs 3:5, TM).

- **Obey your Creator.** Quit trying to do things your way and start doing things God's way—you'll love the end result. "You must obey my laws and be careful to follow my decrees. I am the LORD your God" (Leviticus 18:4).

- **Learn to be a lover of God's Word.** As the butterfly yearns for the sweet nectar of a flower, hunger and thirst for a banquet of spiritual nourishment found only in the Bible. "Anyone who drinks the water I give will never thirst—not ever. The water I give will be an artesian spring within, gushing fountains of endless life" (John 4:14, TM).

- **Keep your new heart in good shape.** When the butterfly emerges, it struggles to remove itself from the cocoon. This strenuous process stimulates the flow of blood into the butterfly's wings and strengthens them for flight. Spiritual exercise keeps our *kardia* muscles toned and in working order. "Stay clear of silly stories that get dressed up as religion. Exercise daily in God—no spiritual flabbiness, please! Workouts in the gymnasium are useful, but a disciplined life in God is far more so, making you fit both today and forever. You can count on this. Take it to heart" (1 Timothy 4:7-9, TM).

A life transformed is a new life with a new heart and a new spirit powered by the Holy Spirit. Your new heart is a gift from God, so be thankful and rejoice! Place your hope in the present and future.

Embrace Hope

Many times the adversary tempted Mom to doubt, to hold back, to fall back to her old ways, to think, *I'm not going to make it.* But she held on to God's plan for her life while focusing her attention on a new rainbow of hope. I watched in amazement how her new hope transformed every aspect of her attitude. Her tomorrows bore no resemblance to her yesterdays. Her faith in God and the loving discipleship of Salvation Army officers enabled her to shatter old habits, wash away old resentments and hurts, discard old fears and limitations, and live a joy-filled life hemmed with grace-filled faith and hope.

Where there is genuine hope, there is the potential for an abundant, victorious life! John Piper writes, "Our hope is when God has promised that something is going to happen and you put your trust in that promise. Christian hope is a confidence that something will come to pass because God has promised it will come to past."[2] The acrostic below can help you embrace the fruits of hope.

- **H—Humility.** A virtue produced by hope and faith, humility is an attitude of the heart. It involves understanding your role in this great Kingdom and fulfilling it for God's divine purposes. Welcome humility—you won't think less of yourself; you'll just think more of others. Your attitude of humility will illuminate a godly vulnerability and transparency. Put away pride and arrogance, and give all glory to God for the good in your life. When we finally let go of ourselves (our concerns, anxieties, self-sufficiency, pride) and give God control of our lives, then, and only then, will we experience humility. Purposely seek humility by having a constant reverence for God, learning to be content in all things, and taming your tongue. Keep a spiritual journal, daily if possible. Write down thoughts and actions that can hinder your realization of a humble attitude.

* * *

What makes humility so desirable is the marvelous thing it does to us; it creates in us a capacity for the closest possible intimacy with God.
—Monica Baldwin

* * *

- **O—Optimism.** Optimism is linked with faith, hope, perseverance, and self-control. An optimistic attitude focuses on the good in others and situations. Optimism doesn't mean viewing the world with unrealistic rose-colored glasses. It means seeing by faith God's hand in your situation and adjusting your attitude accordingly. Learn to use upbeat words. If you wake up in the morning gritting your teeth, make a conscious decision to thank God for allowing you to wake up. Counter negative thoughts with positive thoughts. Focus on right solutions rather than problems.
- **P—Perseverance.** An attitude of perseverance doesn't give up easily or quickly. Remember: the great oak is a little nut that held its ground. Commit yourself to goals, hard work, patience, and endurance. Perseverance involves persisting in the right direction for the long haul. It means standing strong

during the storms with God as your soul anchor. Perseverance and determination cultivate godly character and integrity. Discipline yourself to remain consistent, strong, and diligent regardless of what others say or do. Hope makes dismal days tolerable, because it promises a better tomorrow.

- **E—Enthusiasm.** No one can force enthusiasm on you, because it does not come from the outside. It comes from within. In fact, enthusiasm is a gift from God! The Bible uses terms like "zeal," "spiritual fervor," "joy," and "love." Think about people's excitement for sports, movies, and other types of entertainment. It's always external. The word *enthusiasm* comes from two Greek words: "en," and "theos," which mean to be moved or motivated by God from within by His Holy Spirit. That means enthusiasm results when God works in our lives. How exciting is that? An enthusiastic attitude comes when you receive the truth of God's Word, when you accept God's love, when you allow Him to work in and through you. Let your enthusiasm shine as you worship, encourage others, and live your life with passion and purpose.

It takes deep faith, abundant hope, and discipline to thrive as a transformed child of God. This transformation process you've committed to will bring about vital attitude changes that enable you to realize a new you in proportions beyond your comprehension.

Mom passed away more than twenty years ago. While I dearly miss her, I'm profoundly grateful that the Lord restored our mother-daughter relationship by transforming both of us. Forgiving Mom for the traumas of my childhood has been a long, healing journey, and I won't minimize it. In fact, in my book *Set Free* I write about God's healing power for childhood abuse survivors in order to help victims experience long-lasting healing as well as freedom from their pasts. But today I hold on to the loving memories God has so graciously emblazoned within my heart. Most important, I know for certain that Soldier Bertha Gower is dancing with the angels in heaven.

Dance with Jesus today! Enthusiastically accept God's surrender invitation, let the Great Physician continually renew your heart, and embrace His everlasting hope. He will transform you from the inside out. I know.

Write your thoughts about what you've read.

_____

_____

_____

_____

Questions

1. I hope Mom's story blessed you. Describe your thoughts and emotions when you discovered that Bertha was my mother.

_____

_____

2. Watchmen Nee wrote, "God is waiting until you cease to do. God is waiting for your store of strength to be utterly exhausted before he can deliver you. Once you have ceased to struggle, he will do everything."

How do these words apply to your life?

_____

_____

3. What is holding you back from giving God free reign in your life?

_____

_____

4. "I will give you a new heart, put a new spirit in you. I'll remove the stone heart from your body and replace it with a heart that's God-willed, not self-willed. I'll put my Spirit in you and make it possible for you to do what I tell you and live by my commands" (Ezekiel 36:26-27, TM). Read these verses to yourself several times. Close your eyes and pray for God to give you a new heart. Describe the ways this special gift of a new heart can help transform you from the inside out.

_____

_____

5. In the "Embrace Hope" section of this chapter, I wrote about humility. To help you get started with a spiritual journal, write down thoughts and actions that currently hinder your realization of a humble attitude.

_____

_____

6. What can you do on a daily basis to thrive as a transformed child of God?

_____

_____

10 ✹ BECOME A DIFFERENCE-MAKER IN GOD'S KINGDOM

Act as if what you do makes a difference. It does.

—William James

"What's your name?" I asked.

"Mrs. Juanita King."

"What do you want me to call you?"

"You can call me Mrs. King," she said with a reserved smile.

I sat on the living room sofa with my six-year-old arms folded in front of my chest and stared at Mrs. King, the tall woman with mahogany skin Dad had hired to help around the house while Mom once again received in-patient treatment at a mental hospital. As Mrs. King swept the kitchen, she didn't curse or yell when the broom bristles brushed up against the jelly smeared on the linoleum floor. She simply hummed songs I had heard in church. She set the broom aside and gently moistened a cloth to wipe the sticky section of the floor. Rather than stomp her feet when she walked, she nearly waltzed from room to room.

Maybe this Mrs. Juanita King is different, I thought.

She arrived at our home by 7:00 A.M. Mondays through Fridays and left at 6:00 P.M. I didn't say much at first; I just closely watched her while keeping a safe distance. During her second week on the job, she still waltzed and hummed. A couple of times she caught me peeking around the corner at her; I could tell, because she tilted her head and warmly glanced at me.

One day after school I noticed Mrs. King sitting at the kitchen table with a laundry basket of clean clothes still warm from the dryer. She invited me to help her fold them.

"Where do you go when you leave my house?"

"I go to my home," she said.

"Do you have a family?"

"Yes, I have a husband and two children. My daughter, Raiseen, is six years old, just like you."

"Do you think Raiseen would be my friend?"

"Oh, I'm sure she'd like to be your friend," she said, teasing me with a grin.

My heart danced at the thought of having a friend my own age. I leaned forward and peered into her eyes.

"Can I meet Raiseen?"

"Sure, honey. I'll visit with your dad."

Mrs. King's husband and Dad had known each other for several years, so when Mrs. King asked Dad if I could go home with her the following Friday, he agreed.

Mrs. King held my hand throughout the bus ride and the two-block walk to her home. Her kindness saturated me with special joy. Raiseen grinned ear to ear as her mom introduced us. We skipped through the house, holding hands and singing silly songs. After dinner Mrs. King said, "Time for you two young ladies to bathe!" She didn't point out that my hair was dirty or that my body smelled of urine from wetting the bed. She simply said, "You first, Janice Marie."

I couldn't remember the last time someone had washed my hair or actually showed me how to properly use soap and a washcloth. Mrs. King even handed me a soft towel to dry my sparkling clean body. After our baths, I asked Mrs. King to fix my hair like Raiseen's. She nodded her head and motioned me to the chair in her bedroom where she tenderly braided my damp hair. She clipped several colorful barrettes to my braids. Raiseen and I looked in the mirror and giggled with delight.

"We're twins!" I gleefully declared.

"Well, Honey, in God's eyes you and Raiseen are sisters!"

I proudly became a member of Mrs. King's family a couple of days each month for nearly one year. God knew I needed a surrogate mom in my life, so He delivered this remarkable lady to our home under the pretense of "housekeeper."

Mrs. King didn't intentionally set out to change an abused child's life, but she intentionally loved God and let Him work in and through her. More than fifty years later, I can still visualize her bright chestnut eyes and her endearing smile. More important, her legacy of love and compassion is imprinted on my heart—it lives within me. As I write this chapter and recognize her impact on my life, my soul overflows with the love of Jesus.

God created each of His children to be vessels of love. Like Mrs. King, we can choose to pour out that love to others. Sadly, though, many of us choose to do nothing with it. Since we're fellow sojourners in this adventure, let's accept our godly obligation to make a lasting, positive impact in this negative world. Mother Teresa said, "We can do no great things, only small things with great love." Remember—it's not the one big thing we do in a lifetime; it's all the little things we do, think, and say that create a positive influence with eternal value.

Start today! Practice making a difference right where you are. Create a legacy by leaving a positive imprint with eternal value daily, hourly, and moment by moment. Give God full reign in your *kardia*. Let the Lord minister through you for His kingdom plans and purposes, and you will—

• Let your light so shine

- Pass your positive attitude forward
- Live your life to the fullest

Are you ready to deliberately invest your godly, positive attitude into the lives of others? If so, pray the prayer below:

Lord, help me intentionally let you minister through me so I can learn how to do little things with your love. Help me experience the power of a sincere smile, the rewards of extending a warm hug, and the positive ripple effect of an encouraging word. Make me a vessel of your love. In Jesus' name I pray. Amen.

Let Your Light So Shine

Recently I spoke at a women's retreat in Oklahoma where several hundred ladies gathered to learn and grow, fellowship with one another, and participate in fun activities. Julie, a lady in her early forties, was scheduled to share her testimony ahead of my message for the Saturday evening session.

Because Julie sat next to me on the front row of the conference room, we had an opportunity to introduce ourselves prior to the opening praise-and-worship time. I asked if I could pray for her before she spoke.

"Yes. Please pray that people don't judge me by my past. Pray that Jesus shines from my heart."

I placed an arm around her shoulder and prayed for her. She smiled, flashing her eight or nine remaining teeth, and profusely thanked me.

Julie walked cautiously up to the platform. Her initial nervousness caused the handwritten notes she carried to quiver. She spoke about the emotional pain of aborting her first child conceived when she was a teenager. With hands still trembling, she then recalled her fifteen years of darkness that spiraled downward into a life of prostitution and drug addiction. She paused for a brief moment before continuing. Tears filled her eyes as her demeanor changed. She looked at the audience with confidence and composure as she explained how God had rescued her from a life of self-destruction, then redeemed and transformed her.

"I've been clean, sober, and free for more than ten years."

She laid her notes on the podium and walked to stand in front of it.

"Ten years ago, a kind person told me that Jesus loves me without conditions. This woman walked beside me during my drug addiction recovery. She helped me learn how to study the Bible. She prayed with me regularly. Thanks to her love and kindness, I accepted Jesus as my Lord and Savior nine and a half years ago. Today I teach Bible studies with this lady who befriended me all those years ago."

Julie wiped grateful tears from her eyes while maintaining eye contact with the audience.

* * *

Too often we underestimate the power of a touch,
a smile, a kind word, a listening ear, an honest compliment,
or the smallest act of caring: all of which have
the potential to turn a life around.
—Leo Buscaglia

* * *

"I have a wonderful husband and three beautiful children. We're a dedicated Christian family and very active in our church. My life Bible verse is Philippians 4:13—'I can do everything through him who gives me strength.'"

The audience stood up and encouraged her with a grand applause.

After my presentation, the Lord spoke to my heart as clearly as if He had said the words aloud.

Jan, give Julie your silver bracelet.

I sat next to Julie while a soloist sang. I stroked my bracelet and read the engraved words: "I can do everything through him who gives me strength" (Philippians 4:13). After the final song, Julie and I talked privately. I reached for her hand and slipped the bracelet onto her wrist, saying, "This is a gift from Jesus!"

She cried some more and hugged me really big.

"God answered your prayers, Julie," I said. "Your testimony touched the heart of every woman present tonight. You let your light so shine."

Julie exemplified Jesus' words—

Here's another way to put it: You're here to be light, bringing out the God-colors in the world. God is not a secret to be kept. We're going public with this, as public as a city on a hill. If I make you light-bearers, you don't think I'm going to hide you under a bucket, do you? I'm putting you on a light stand. Now that I've put you there on a hilltop, on a light stand—shine! Keep open house; be generous with your lives. By opening up to others, you'll prompt people to open up with God, this generous Father in heaven *(Matthew 5:14-16, TM)*.

When we live for Jesus, we glow like lights, showing others who Jesus is and what He is like. How can you let your light so shine? You can be a beacon of light, and here's how:

- Live for Jesus.
- Walk the walk with a smile on your face and a light in your heart.
- Let Jesus minister through you.
- Be vulnerable and transparent.
- Extend loving-kindness to others.

- Use words of encouragement.
- Share your testimony to point others to the One who redeems and restores.

We are walking advertisements for Jesus. As you shine for Jesus, never underestimate the power of one! Remember—Jesus fed five thousand people from one young boy's five loaves of bread and two small fish.

Pass Your Positive Attitude Forward

Several years ago I spoke at The Salvation Army International Social Services Conference in Canada. The officers listened intently as I described my childhood. Glancing into the audience, I noticed white tissues dabbing tears. I thanked the officers for giving me a mother while painting a brief picture of Mom's last season of life and how God worked through the Army to give Mom a new life.

After my presentation Major Ruth stopped me in the hotel hallway.

"You mentioned Kansas City, Missouri, in your presentation," she said. "Is that where your mother lived?"

"Yes."

"Do you mind me asking your mother's name?"

"Bertha Gower."

Major Ruth paused. She grabbed my right hand and squeezed it gently. Tears streaked her face.

"I've often wondered what happened to Bertha. I'm the woman who picked her up for Bible study and meals."

We hugged. We cried. We rejoiced. The Lord knit our hearts together during this divine encounter.

Major Ruth explained to me that Salvation Army policy requires officers to move to different areas around the country frequently. As a result, officers rarely get to see the end results of their labor. They might get a glimpse of a person's transformation but seldom the final "butterfly." For reasons beyond my comprehension, this time God allowed Major Ruth to see firsthand the fruits of her labor.

Throughout the next two days of this conference, officers from all corners of the world thanked me for encouraging them by sharing my testimony as well as Mom's final triumph. Several officers mentioned that my words refueled their weary souls and made them realize that what they do matters in the grand eternal scheme of things.

* * *

The only gift is a portion of thyself.

—Ralph Waldo Emerson

* * *

These brave servants didn't realize that their positive feedback energized me and filled me with the passion to continue pressing on during a difficult speaking and writing season of my life. That's the way God works! The more we intentionally or unintentionally pass our godly, positive perspective forward, the deeper the blessings we receive. Some people use the phrase "pay it forward," coined from a movie that was titled with those same words. This film chronicled a seventh-grader's ingenious plan to make a difference in the world. I choose to say "pass it forward," because in this context I refer to making a difference in the lives of others simply by extravagantly giving others what we already have: a great attitude.

We're all soldiers for Christ, striving to make a difference in the lives of others. How can you "pass forward" your positive perspective in order to make a difference in someone's life? The "GIVE" acrostic that propels your positive perspective into action by helping others.

- **Generate Generosity.** The best way to generate generosity in others is to give of yourself. Freely give kindness, patience, understanding, and love. Start by being generous with your life. Jesus said, "Give away your life; you'll find life given back, but not merely given back—given back with bonus and blessing. Giving, not getting, is the way. Generosity begets generosity" (Luke 6:38, TM).

- **Inspire.** Let your positive perspective flow through your words and actions to inspire others to become the people God created them to be. Let others see Jesus in you! "Let every detail in your lives—words, actions, whatever—be done in the name of the Master, Jesus, thanking God the Father every step of the way" (Colossians 3:17, TM).

* * *

People who inspire others are those who see invisible bridges at the end of dead-end streets.
—Chuck Swindoll

* * *

- **Volunteer.** Don't wait to be recruited; instead, look for serving opportunities to enhance the lives of others. Generously give of your time, even if you never get a thank-you. Let the Lord guide your steps as you find a need, and fill it. "Here is a simple, rule-of-thumb guide for behavior: Ask yourself what you want people to do for you, then grab the initiative and do it for them" (Matthew 7:12, TM).

- **Encourage.** Strengthen and encourage the weary, the lonely, the downhearted. "Learn to do right! Seek justice, encourage the oppressed. Defend the cause of the fatherless, plead the case of the widow" (Isaiah 1:17).

The next time you shop at Wal-Mart, pay close attention to the greeters who make it a top priority to greet customers with a friendly smile and a verbal welcome. Most greeters are senior citizens with a positive attitude who truly enjoy helping and interacting with people. The friendly greeters literally set a good example for us to follow: Pass our positive attitudes forward!

Live Your New Life to the Fullest

Throughout the pages of this book I've opened up my heart to you. You know my past heartaches, my downfalls, my weaknesses. You also know the miraculous wonders God has done in my life. King David's psalm sums up my life quite well: "He lifted me out of the ditch, pulled me from deep mud. He stood me up on a solid rock to make sure I wouldn't slip. He taught me how to sing the latest God-song, a praise-song to our God" (Psalm 40:2-3, TM). The Bible promises that when people see drastic change in our lives, they'll be astounded to the point of placing their trust in God. We're difference-makers in God's kingdom. Believe it! Live it!

If anyone had told me thirty years ago that God planned a life immersed in full-time ministry for me, I would have rolled my eyes, tossed my head, and said, "Yeah, right." I'm living proof that God does not discriminate. He loves a challenge.

Guess what. God has grand designs with eternal value for our lives. These plans include a life surrendered to Jesus, a guarantee of starting each moment with a new beginning, and living our positive new life to the fullest. If that's as good as it gets here on Planet Earth, I'll take it. How about you?

I pray my vulnerability and transparency inspire you to peel off the layers of self-consciousness, fear, and insecurities that can stifle living your new life.

The apostle Paul says, "You're done with that old life. It's like a filthy set of ill-fitting clothes you've stripped off and put in the fire. Now you're dressed in a new wardrobe. Every item of your new way of life is custom-made by the Creator, with his label on it" (Colossians 3:10, TM).

Yes, you're brand new. So kick up your heels and dance with joy. You are a custom-designed daughter of the King—a princess in God's kingdom. Granted, if you're anything like me, you may have to hold on to your crown to keep it from slipping from time to time. The good news: We're all works-in-progress, and until we stand face to face with Jesus, we'll continue to grow from the inside out.

Thank you for the honor of walking beside you as you discover how to apply the positive attitude secrets to your life. Hold dear the true stories within the pages of this book. Reread the book, and then pass it forward to a friend or family member. Never forget the value and importance of your ability to—

1. Create and preserve a positive attitude.

2. Respond to change rather than react.

3. Maintain personal accountability.

4. Invite God to search your heart.

5. Forgive others, and accept God's forgiveness of yourself.

6. Face and overcome obstacles.

7. Learn to give and receive love.

8. Take charge of your thoughts.

9. Transform from a caterpillar to a butterfly.

10. Become a difference-maker whom God can use.

As you journey forward in your new life, I ask that you let me know how you've been able to incorporate the ten secrets into your life as well as how you've made a difference in the life of another person. Feel free to e-mail me at jan@jancoates.com, or visit my web site at <www.jancoates.com>. If you want to be my Facebook friend, send a friend invite to Jan Coates.

Until we meet face to face, I give you the prayer below from my heart to yours.

God, I thank you for the privilege of holding the hands and hearts of all the precious readers throughout this positivity journey. I ask that you richly bless them while guiding and directing their every step. Fill them with a lasting passion to see the world through your sovereign eyes as they live each day to the fullest. Thank you for all that you're going to do through them. In Christ's name I pray. Amen.

One last thing: don't forget to read the bonus chapter, chapter eleven, which features a complete positive attitude tool kit to help you motivate yourself as you maintain, personalize, and fine-tune the secrets you've discovered in this book.

Write your thoughts about what you've read.

_____

_____

_____

_____

_____

_____

Questions

1. Have you ever known someone like Mrs. King? If so, what positive impact did that person have in your life?

_____

_____

2. Mother Teresa said, "We can do no great things, only small things with great love." How can you apply this truth to your life?

_____

_____

3. How did Julie let her light so shine?

_____

_____

4. What can you do today to let your light so shine?

_____

_____

5. How can you give generously of yourself to make a difference in God's kingdom?

_____

_____

6. God has grand plans with eternal value for your life. How does that make you feel?

_____

_____

11 ✺ BONUS CHAPTER
Your Positivity Tool Kit

You did it!

Congratulations! You have successfully completed *Attitude-in-ize*. To help you forge ahead and personalize the positive perspective secrets contained in this book, I thought it appropriate to include a "Positivity Tool Kit" for your reflection, as well as blank lines for your input.

Your godly positivity potential is limited only by your level of commitment to what you've learned in this book and intentionally apply to your life. Like the other ten chapters, this chapter exemplifies positivity from a godly, biblical viewpoint as you discover ways to motivate yourself.

This interactive chapter includes the following keys to sustain your positive perspective progress:

- Ask the right questions.
- Establish goals.
- Compile godly affirmations.
- Create a positivity scrapbook.
- Build a support team.
- Memorize scripture.

Ask the Right Questions

Jesus, our Savior and perfect mentor, incorporated questions in His communications to provoke thinking in a way that statements do not. The Gospels record more than one hundred questions asked by Jesus. Here are several to demonstrate my point.

- "Let me tell you why you are here. You're here to be salt-seasoning that brings out the God-flavors of this earth. If you lose your saltiness, how will people taste godliness?" (Matthew 5:13, TM).

- "Therefore I tell you, do not worry about your life, what you will eat or drink; or about your body, what you will wear. Is not life more important than food, and the body more important than clothes?" (Matthew 6:25).

- "Why do you look at the speck of sawdust in your brother's eye and pay no attention to the plank in your own eye?" (Matthew 7:3).

See what I mean? Jesus' questions call for deep reflection and a reply.

While our ability to ask questions is a key communication skill, asking ourselves questions can actually help us create and maintain a positive perspective. Questions allow you to shift your focus and view situations from a different slant. The questions outlined below will help you radiate positivity. Write in the space provided or in your journal.

1. What small thing am I thankful to God for?

_____

_____

2. What big thing am I thankful to God for?

_____

_____

3. How has God blessed my life?

_____

_____

4. What is the beauty surrounding my home, apartment, office, community?

_____

_____

5. What good happened in my life today? (Hint: Did you wake up?)

_____

_____

6. What good is going on in my life now?

_____

_____

7. Whom do I appreciate and why?

_____

_____

8. Who appreciates me and why?

_____

_____

9. What memory brings a smile to my face?

_____

_____

Shifting the slant of a negative experience can stimulate a positive perspective. Answer the following questions as you practice this technique of finding a positive meaning in your challenging circumstances.

10. What can I learn from this experience?

_____

_____

11. The Bible promises that "We can be so sure that every detail in our lives of love for God is worked into something good" (Romans 8:28, TM). How will God in His perfect time use this situation for my good?

_____

_____

_____

12. Who can I help as a result of this experience?

_____

_____

13. What do I need to change about me?

_____

_____

14. I reacted rather than thoughtfully responding. What insight have I gained that will help me in future situations?

_____

_____

Establish Goals

It is important to set positive attitude goals and plans that our hearts, souls, and minds can conceive, believe, and carry out. Our biblically sound goals help us achieve measurable short-term and long-term objectives.

SMART, a commonly used acronym, provides great guidelines

for goal-setting. While there are plenty of variants, SMART typically stands for—

- **Specific**: Set specific goals. For example, "I want to make a difference in someone's life" is too generic. Rather, "I'm going to send a handwritten note of appreciation to _____ this afternoon" is specific.

- **Measurable**: Attach a measurable qualification to each goal. For example, "I'm going to smile and speak encouraging words to at least three people at work today."

- **Achievable**: Keep goals reasonable and achievable. For example, "I want to forgive everyone who has wronged me in my lifetime within the next fifteen minutes" is an overzealous approach to forgiveness. The fifth secret to a new you explains that forgiving someone who deeply hurt you can sometimes be a lengthy process between you and God. A reasonable and achievable forgiveness goal would be "I'm going to ask God to help me talk about the pain caused by _____ for _____."

- **Relevant**: Keep your goals relevant and in accordance to God's plans and purposes for your life. For example, "I'm going to take charge of my negative thoughts by giving them to God."

- **Time Frame**: Have a set time to reach your goal in order to fuel your goals with structure. It also helps you monitor your progress. For example, "On the way home from work I'm going to thank God for helping me adjust my perspective."

Now that you know the fundamentals of goal-setting, keep the SMART acronym in mind to help you remember the basics. The following is a worksheet to help you get started.

Goal Worksheet[1]

Today's Date: _____ Target Date: _____

Start Date: _____ Date Achieved: _____

Goal: _____

Specific: What exactly will you accomplish?

_____

_____

Measurable: How will you know when you have reached the goal? _____

_____

Achievable: Is achieving this goal reasonable?

_____

_____

Relevant: How is the goal relevant to your new life?

_____

_____

Time Frame: When will this goal be realized?

_____

_____

Here are four encouraging Bible verses that reinforce the importance of godly goals and plans.

- "Put GOD in charge of your work, then what you've planned will take place" (Proverbs 16:3, TM).
- "We plan the way we want to live, but only GOD makes us able to live it" (Proverbs 16:9, TM).

- "I press on toward the goal to win the prize for which God has called me heavenward in Christ Jesus" (Philippians 3:14).

- "'I know the plans I have for you,' declares the LORD, 'plans to prosper you and not to harm you, plans to give you hope and a future'" (Jeremiah 29:11).

Compile Godly Affirmations

An affirmation is a positive statement to reinforce or change thinking patterns. It's a law of nature that what you keep in your *kardia* determines the outcome of your experiences. Focus on the negative, and you'll find yourself in a downward spiral filled with *should haves, could haves,* and the dreaded *if onlys.* By focusing on the positive, you can overcome the negative.

Affirmations consist of lists you compose—Bible verses as well as quotations. Use the following sample to help you get the feel for positive, uplifting lists; then use the blank "My Personal Affirmation List" to compile your own lists.

Sample List

Description	List
Five of my strengths include—	1. Faith in God 2. Positive perspective 3. Kindness 4. Compassion 5. Gentleness
Three of my recent accomplishments include—	1. I pray and read the Bible before making decisions. 2. I respond to change rather than react. 3. Today I replaced my excuses with fresh determination.

My Personal Affirmation List

Description	List
Five of my strengths include—	1. 2. 3. 4. 5.
Three of my recent accomplishments include—	1. 2. 3.
Five things I can do to help my family and friends—	1. 2. 3. 4. 5.
Three positive choices I've made this week—	1. 2. 3.
Today I said kind, encouraging words to—	1. 2. 3.
Recently I said no to negativity by—	1. 2.

Regular use of affirmation lists will help keep your inner growth heading in the right direction. Get creative, and add your own affirmations to your list. Let God speak to your heart through these Bible affirmations. Try reading them aloud.

Positive Affirmations[2]

- "I am full with the joy of the Lord" (see Isaiah 42:10).
- "I am fearfully and wonderfully made by God" (see Psalm 139:14).
- "I have rest in my soul because I go to Jesus when I am weary" (Matthew 11:28-29).

- "I can never be separated from the love of God" (see Romans 8:35-39).
- "With God in my life, all things are possible." (see Matthew 19:26).
- "God is for me so no one can ever be against me" (see Romans 8:31).
- "God meets all my needs" (see Philippians 4:19).
- "God satisfies me when I am thirsty and fills me with good things when I am hungry" (see Psalm 107:9).
- "I display a new nature because I am a new person, created in God's likeness" (see Ephesians 4:24).
- "I can do anything because I believe" (see Mark 11:24).
- "I am content" (see Philippians 4:11).
- "I am at peace" (see John 14:27).
- "I have life to the fullest" (see John 10:10).
- "The Lord renews my strength. I soar on wings like eagles" (see Isaiah 40:31).
- "I am chosen" (see Ephesians 1:11).
- "I have a *new life*" (see 2 Corinthians 5:17).

Make a Positivity Scrapbook

Buy a scrapbook and label it "Positivity." You can decoratively place anything in it that invigorates you. Get creative by using colored paper, stickers, and weird-cutting scissors. With a little effort this could be a work of art. Here are some items I stick in my scrapbook:

- Inspirational quotes
- Hand-written notes and e-mails from readers and speaking audiences
- Silly pictures of my family
- Bible verses

- Action photos of my two kittens, Zeke and Zoë
- Birthday and Mother's Day cards from hubby and kids
- Short affirmation lists
- Printed copies of completed "to do". lists
- Printed copies of achieved goals
- Photos from magazines and newspapers that make me giggle

Keep your scrapbook in a convenient place so you can browse through it when you need a positivity boost.

Build a Support Team

Surround yourself with upbeat people you know, like, and trust. If you're not already involved in a small group at your church, join one. Christian small groups stimulate close relationships while providing prayer support and positive interaction. Also, consider joining a Bible study at your church where you'll meet a wide variety of delightful friends. If you're a career person, think about local organizations that maintain your core values.

I've personally found organizations like American Business Women's Association to be a delightful group of uplifting, professional ladies. The members are fun and energized and have a wealth of experience to share with others. If you're a mom with young children, consider joining Mothers of Preschoolers (MOPS). MOPS features regular meetings with encouraging support for moms with similar interests. Stonecroft Ministries offers Women's Connections and Christian Women's Clubs. They meet monthly over brunch, lunch, or dinner. Each event includes an entertaining feature and an inspirational speaker who offers insight on how to have a personal relationship with Jesus. Stonecroft provides an opportunity for women of all ages to meet new friends, get involved, and join the weekly Bible studies. The keywords in building a support team: "Get involved."

When you join or start a support team, don't ask what's in it for you. Tweak your attitude to think, *What can I contribute to this group?* By getting involved and giving of yourself, you'll discover the rewards of team positivity dynamics. In other words, the more you give the more you receive. In his book *The Purpose Driven Life* Rick Warren says, "Study without service leads to spiritual stagnation. The old comparison between the Sea of Galilee and the Dead Sea is still true. Galilee is a lake full of life because it takes in water but also gives it out. In contrast, nothing lives in the Dead Sea because, with no outflow, the lake has stagnated."[1]

For online positivity interaction, connect with me at Facebook or my website, at <www.jancoates.com>. I post encouraging words daily as well as thought-provoking questions.

Doodle some creative ideas on the form below that will help you build a positive support team.

Organization	Team/Group	My Contribution

Memorize Scripture

Memorizing scripture refreshes your *kardia* by filling it with truth. When you commit to scripture memorization, you initiate the process of minimizing negative forces in your life by replacing them with divine power and potential of God's promises.

The verses below are worthy of memorization.

- "Trust in the LORD with all your heart and lean not on your own understanding" (Proverbs 3:5).
- "God, you are my God" (Isaiah 25:1, TM).
- "For God so loved the world that he gave his one and only Son, that whoever believes in him shall not perish but have eternal life" (John 3:16).
- "Do not let any unwholesome talk come out of your mouths, but only what is helpful for building others up" (Ephesians 4:29).
- "Be imitators of God" (Ephesians 5:1).
- "Be kind and compassionate to one another, forgiving each other, just as in Christ God forgave you" (Ephesians 4:32).
- "I can do all things through him who gives me strength" (Philippians 4:13).
- "Do not grieve, for the joy of the LORD is your strength" (Nehemiah 8:10).
- "Giving, not getting, is the way. Generosity begets generosity" (Luke 6:38, TM).

Your turn! Make a list in the form below of Bible verses you desire to commit to memory.

My Bible Memory Verses

Verse Text	Bible Reference

My prayer is that your scripture memorization list grows as you bask in and spread God's love, joy, and peace throughout your life. God bless you, my friend!

APPENDIX

Father's Love Letter

My Child,
You may not know me,
but I know everything about you.
Psalm 139:1

I know when you sit down and when you rise up.
Psalm 139:2

I am familiar with all your ways.
Psalm 139:3

Even the very hairs on your head are numbered.
Matthew 10:29-31

For you were made in my image.
Genesis 1:27

In me you live and move and have your being.
Acts 17:28

For you are my offspring.
Acts 17:28

I knew you even before you were conceived.
Jeremiah 1:4-5

I chose you when I planned creation.
Ephesians 1:11-12

You were not a mistake,
for all your days are written in my book.
Psalm 139:15-16

I determined the exact time of your birth
and where you would live.
Acts 17:26

You are fearfully and wonderfully made.
Psalm 139:14

I knit you together in your mother's womb.
Psalm 139:13

And brought you forth on the day you were born.
Psalm 71:6

I have been misrepresented
by those who don't know me.
John 8:41-44

I am not distant and angry,
but am the complete expression of love.
1 John 4:16

And it is my desire to lavish my love on you.
1 John 3:1

Simply because you are my child
and I am your Father.
1 John 3:1

I offer you more than your earthly father ever could.
Matthew 7:11

For I am the perfect father.
Matthew 5:48

Every good gift that you receive comes from my hand.
James 1:17

For I am your provider and I meet all your needs.
Matthew 6:31-33

My plan for your future has always been filled with hope.
Jeremiah 29:11

Because I love you with an everlasting love.
Jeremiah 31:3

My thoughts toward you are countless
as the sand on the seashore.
Psalms 139:17-18

And I rejoice over you with singing.
Zephaniah 3:17

I will never stop doing good to you.
Jeremiah 32:40

For you are my treasured possession.
Exodus 19:5

I desire to establish you
with all my heart and all my soul.
Jeremiah 32:41

And I want to show you great and marvelous things.
Jeremiah 33:3

If you seek me with all your heart,
you will find me.
Deuteronomy 4:29

Delight in me and I will give you
the desires of your heart.
Psalm 37:4

For it is I who gave you those desires.
Philippians 2:13

I am able to do more for you
than you could possibly imagine.
Ephesians 3:20

For I am your greatest encourager.
2 Thessalonians 2:16-17

I am also the Father who comforts you
in all your troubles.
2 Corinthians 1:3-4

When you are brokenhearted,
I am close to you.
Psalm 34:18

As a shepherd carries a lamb,
I have carried you close to my heart.
Isaiah 40:11

One day I will wipe away
every tear from your eyes.
Revelation 21:3-4

And I'll take away all the pain
you have suffered on this earth.
Revelation 21:3-4

I am your Father, and I love you
even as I love my son, Jesus.
John 17:23

For in Jesus, my love for you is revealed.
John 17:26

He is the exact representation of my being.
Hebrews 1:3

He came to demonstrate that I am for you,
not against you.
Romans 8:31

And to tell you that I am not counting your sins.
2 Corinthians 5:18-19

Jesus died so that you and I could be reconciled.
2 Corinthians 5:18-19

His death was the ultimate expression
of my love for you.
1 John 4:10

I gave up everything I loved
that I might gain your love.
Romans 8:31-32

If you receive the gift of my son Jesus,
you receive me.
1 John 2:23

And nothing will ever separate you
from my love again.
Romans 8:38-39

Come home and I'll throw the biggest party
heaven has ever seen.
Luke 15:7

I have always been Father,
and will always be Father.
Ephesians 3:14-15

My question is . . .
Will you be my child?
John 1:12-13

I am waiting for you.
Luke 15:11-32
Love, Your Dad
Almighty God

"Father's Love Letter," used by permission of Father Heart Communications. Copyright 1999-2010. <www.fathersloveletter.com>

NOTES

Introduction

1. John C. Maxwell, *The Winning Attitude* (Nashville: Thomas Nelson, 1993), 30.

Chapter 1

1. <http://thinkexist.com/quotation/motivation-is-a-fire-from-within-if-someone-else/362837.html>

2. Charles R. Swindoll, *Strengthening Your Grip* (Waco, TX: Word, 1988), 301.

Chapter 3

1. Tommy Newberry, *The 4:8 Principle* (Carol Stream, Ill.: Tyndale House Publishers, 2007), xiv.

Chapter 5

1. Oswald Chambers, *My Utmost for His Highest* (Grand Rapids: Discovery, 1992), December 7.

2. Chambers, *My Utmost for His Highest*, November 20.

Chapter 6

1. <http://www.brainyquote.com/quotes/quotes/b/billygraham50666.html>.

2. <http://en.wikipedia.org/wiki/GeorgeMueller, <http://www.desiringgod.org/ResourceLibrary/Biographies/1531/>. George Muellers Strategy for Showing God.

3. <http://www.bestavros.net/adel/Home.html>.

Chapter 7

1. "Father's Love Letter," used by permission of Father Heart Communications, copyright 1999-2010. <www.fathersloveletter.com>.

2. Philip Carlson, *You Were Made for Love* (Colorado Springs: Cook Communications, 2006), 79.

Chapter 8

1. Sarah Young, *Jesus Calling* (Nashville: Thomas Nelson, 2004), March 20.

2. Neil T. Anderson, *Who I Am in Christ* (Ventura, Calif.: Regal Books, 1993), 278.

3. A. W. Tozer, *Tozer Topical Reader,* comp. Ron Eggert (Camp Hill, Pa.: Christian Publications, 1998), 1.194.

Chapter 9

1. Watchman Nee, *Sit Stand Walk* (Wheaton, Ill.: Tyndale House Publishers, 1985), 23.

2. <http://www.desiringgod.org/ResourceLibrary/AskPastorJohn/ByTopic/24/2649_What_is_so_important_about_Christian_hope/>.

Chapter 11

1. <www.officearrow.com>, Jason Wernick, modified with permission.

2. <www.faithandhealthconnection.org>, Dale Fletcher.

3. Rick Warren, *The Purpose-Driven Life* (Grand Rapids: Zondervan Publishing House, 2002), 231.

YOU DON'T HAVE TO LIVE WITH A POOR SELF-IMAGE.

This helpful, inspirational book shows you how to see yourself as God sees you and live in peace and joy with eager anticipation for your future. Dr. Helen McIntosh, a licensed counselor, has experienced the emotional anguish and devastation that past hurts can cause. In *Messages to Myself,* she shares with you the methods that you can start using immediately to change the messages you give yourself every day.

MESSAGES TO MYSELF
By Helen B. McIntosh
ISBN: 978-0-8341-2456-1

BEACON HILL PRESS
OF KANSAS CITY

Available online and wherever books are sold.

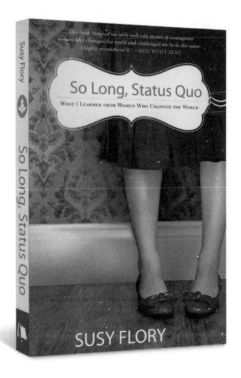